Seeing Seattle

P9-DML-346

Seeing Seattle

ROGER SALE

Photographs by Mary Randlett

University of Washington Press   *Seattle & London*

For David Brewster and Tom Williams

Copyright © 1994 by the University of Washington Press
Printed in the United States of America

All rights reserved. No part of this publication may be reproduced or transmitted in any form or by any means, electronic or mechanical, including photocopy, recording, or any information storage or retrieval system, without permission in writing from the publisher.

Library of Congress Cataloging-in-Publication Data

Sale, Roger.
Seeing Seattle / Roger Sale ; photographs by Mary Randlett.
p. cm.
Includes bibliographical references and index.
ISBN 0-295-97359-5 (pbk. : alk. paper)
1. Seattle (Wash.) Guidebooks. I. Randlett, Mary. II. Title.
F899.S43S25   1994   94-5715
917.97'7720443—dc20   CIP

The paper used in this publication meets the minimum requirements of American National Standard for Information Sciences—Permanence of Paper for Printed Library Materials, ANSI Z39.48–1984.∞

Front matter illustrations
p. 2. Dancers Series: Steps, by Jack Mackie (Capitol Hill)
p. 6. Exchange Building, John Graham, Sr., architect (downtown)

Contents

Foreword

My father, Victor Steinbrueck, wrote in his book *Seattle Cityscape* (1962) that "no one ever fully knows the city because one's perception is always incomplete, subjective, and ever changing." Indeed, the city itself is ever changing. But unlike many other American cities, Seattle is still a wonderful place where one can take a pleasurable walk almost anywhere and see the city.

Seattle is now at a crossroads. Over the past decade, the metropolitan region has experienced unprecedented growth pressures that threaten the quality of life Seattleites have long enjoyed and used to take for granted. Will we, Seattle's citizens, have the concern, foresight, and wherewithal to protect this great city's future from the usual pattern of urban decay caused by rising crime, traffic congestion, poorly designed development, and urban sprawl? What makes for a more livable city?

In our daily lives we must take the time to look more closely at the world around us, and learn from it. Respect for what we have comes with knowing the city more intimately. There is no better way to observe the urban environment than by walking it.

More than the typical banal tourist guide, *Seeing Seattle* is a book "full of opinions and judgments," with insightful commentaries on what is right about Seattle, what is wrong, what has been woefully lost, and what can still be preserved. In short, it's about what is uniquely Seattle. *Seeing Seattle* should be of interest not only to visitors but to those of us who live in and love the city and want to see, experience, and appreciate more of it.

So go see Seattle, but be sure to go by foot, of course!

Peter Steinbrueck
Seattle, March 1994

Acknowledgments

My greatest debt, as will be obvious to anyone who turns even a few of these pages, is to Mary Randlett, who took on the task of illustrating them, if not entirely as a labor of love, then as a labor undertaken lovingly. As we went around Seattle she kept saying, "Tell me what you see," because she *is* an illustrator here. Then I learned much from seeing what she saw, too.

I have never met Arthur Lee Jacobson, whose *Trees of Seattle* accompanied me as I was devising these walks, and who read the book in manuscript and pleased me when he reported that reading it was "never a chore" even as he noted lots of mistakes in my tree identifications. But I loved the feeling that I was bound to run into him in some unlikely spot (E. North St.? N.W. Cleopatra?), and *should* meet him thus.

Dennis Andersen, Fred Bassetti, Ibsen Nelsen, and Peter Steinbrueck also read the book in manuscript, also corrected errors, often wisely urged me to find out a little more, go back and take another look, and were generally generous to one who "doesn't know anything about architecture."

Catherine Allberg, while an intern at *Seattle Weekly,* did much helpful leg and phone work for me. University of Washington's architect, Ed Duthweiler, informed me about University buildings. Assunta Ng, editor of the *Chinese Post,* gave me a perspective on Chinatown/International District I could not otherwise have gained. I received courteous assistance from various people in the city's Historic Preservation office.

Finally, the two good friends, David Brewster and Tom Williams, to whom the book is dedicated. David encouraged me from the time I first conceived this project, and gave me good tryingout space for some of these walks in *Seattle Weekly.* Tom read pages as I wrote them, gave me great brief verbal nudges ("More stories," "Too many notes, Herr Mozart"), and showed me what a native to the city knows that I, a mere thirty year resident, can't know.

Seeing Seattle

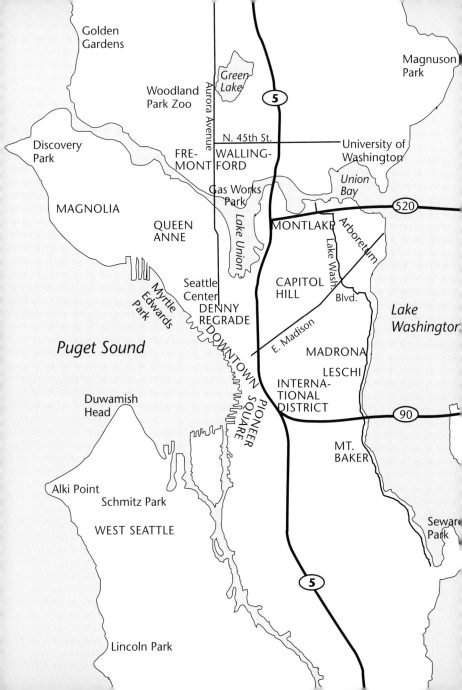

1 Introduction

Most guidebooks to most cities are extensions of the tourist industry, designed to tell visitors how to find the great landmarks, what hours the museums are open, where the fun places are in or near downtown. Seattle has a number of such books, but this is not one of them. Nor is this a restaurant and hotel guide; for that I'd recommend *Seattle Best Places,* revised regularly and as reliable as such books can be.

As its title implies, *Seeing Seattle* is about seeing.

If you are in Seattle only for a day or two, there is probably too much in this book for you, and what is here is too undifferentiated. You will do quite well if you ask your host or hostelier how to get to two or three of the following: Pike Place Market, the signature place; the Space Needle, the signature structure, where you take the elevator to the observation deck; Pioneer Square; the waterfront, where you walk and ride the trolley; Woodland Park Zoo, especially for the African savanna and the gorillas; for the best trees and shrubs, the Arboretum and the University of Washington campus, especially between February and June, and October-November.

If you are in Seattle for any length of time between a week and forever, I hope this book can help create or sustain your interest in the city. There are few serious guidebooks about cities its age (140 years) and size (half a million) and even fewer that are willing to make negative as well as positive judgments; those seem reserved for cities much older and larger. And that is a shame, because Seattle is a marvelous city, full of interesting things to see, quite capable of standing up to close scrutiny and having someone point out what is barren or misshaped as well as what is striking and beautiful. All of us, if we live in the same place for a considerable length of time, get into habits of taking for granted—of not seeing. What I am seeking for my readers is what I found for myself working on this book, namely a sense that when I took my time, made myself see, I discovered much that I was looking at as if for the first time. What I aim for here is seeing as if one were, in Thoreau's terms, quite awake.

I wrote a history of Seattle twenty years ago, *Seattle Past to Present,* and afterward many people asked me to show them around Seattle, as though the local historian might be the best guide. I showed people the routes taken by early railroads, where the fire of 1889 started, old homes, the International District. It never seemed to work. I eventually realized that I had never seriously asked myself to start with the visual and use the historical as supplementary context when and as needed. I also discovered that I was not the only one with this problem. The drivers for Gray Line Tours offer their spiel about Seattle over a two-hour tour, and in peak months they do this three or four times a day. Understandably they get bored with what they are saying, and some years ago their union asked me if I could speak to their problem. I took the tour, and discovered that while the driver was directly relating what the passengers could see with the lore he had memorized, he wasn't really seeing what he was talking about, and he wasn't trying to imagine what his passengers, many of whom came from cities very different from Seattle, could make of what they saw. This was precisely the mistake I made when showing newcomers around.

So what I tried to formulate for myself, and for the Gray Line drivers, was a sense of seeing that involved asking questions of both the lore and what one was seeing. Since the drivers *are* an extension of the tourist industry, they can't say some things without getting into trouble, but that leaves much to be explored. Residential streets, for instance, were almost ignored unless some anecdote accrued to one particular house. But residential streets can be as revealing about a city as landmarks. Some were developed, for instance, with houses that looked to be built at roughly the same time and costing about the same amount, some that were more of a hotchpotch; in some cases the homogeneous street seemed interesting, in some sterile; on the more motley streets, amid a row of older bungalows, a newer, more expensive and pretentious house or two could be found. To note these things leads to questions: Why is that a more attractive row of houses than this? Why would someone build a $200,000 house on a street where its neighbors might cost no more than half that? You could not only ask such questions, but you could ask your passengers to ask them too, and to compare what they were seeing with what they knew at home—where, more likely than not, there would be a much higher percentage of brick and stucco than there is here.

This book is about seeing, then, and discovering what one makes of what one sees—banishing all thought that one has to be an expert. I am not an architect or an architectural critic, nor am I a botanist or a landscape designer. I was not a bona fide urban historian when I wrote *Seattle Past to Present* either. I have had to consult experts in a number of fields to do this book, but I have then moved on to try to see for myself. Along with this I have also insisted to myself that I have preferences and opinions as a way of finding out why I am responding as I am. I have not posited or derived any rules, theories, or principles, because I discovered I could admire a building for its grandeur and not like another equally grand. And something may be good because it is ordinary, but something else only flat or boring in its ordinariness.

Therefore this book is full of opinions and judgments, which I offer as part of a collaborative process in which you look, ask, and form your own opinions and judgments. My favorite guidebook, *Nairn's London,* has many conclusions I do not "agree" with, yet Ian Nairn has made me see more freshly than I knew was possible, and his book has been an inspiration for this one.

Nairn's London offers descriptions, usually about half a page in length, of "the 450 best things" in London. I doubt if even the tourist board or the chamber of commerce could imagine there are "450 best things" in Seattle as befits a city one-tenth as old and as large as London. Forty-five is probably close to the right number. But there is much that is interesting and worth asking about that may not even compute in a competition for "best things." To try to express this I have organized most of the book as walks and drives, and in most of these I have, in addition to looking at what is most striking, tried to derive a theme, a point, a sense of historical event or change, of someone's or something's achievement. Fortunately, most of this book can be covered by someone who has no car. The drives are for more outlying areas where distances between places of note and/or heavy traffic make walking unfeasible or undesirable, and I have indicated bus routes from downtown to any place easily accessible by bus. I have also included estimated times for each walk and drive. This will be of most use to you if you bear in mind that I am a fairly brisk walker, I am not much of a shopper, and with

most places would I prefer to look for five minutes on three con-
secutive days than for fifteen minutes on one. You should have a
Seattle map, preferably one that includes neighborhoods as well
as streets, central Seattle from Seattle Center to Pioneer Square in
detail, and an index to important buildings. My policy, somewhat
reluctantly adopted, is to give the name of each building at the
time of this book's publication in 1994. In the case of buildings
downtown especially, names can change frequently, however, so
that current names may not be the ones by which many know
the buildings, or the ones they may be called as you stand before
them, *Seeing Seattle* in hand. The index includes the original
names of many buildings.

Although, like any guidebook, *Seeing Seattle* is not to be read
through beginning to end, I have written it such that, unless
there was some obvious reason not to, the first significant reference to something that will be mentioned on more than one
walk or drive, like an architect or a useful book, will be the fullest.
I am afraid, however, that there will be many points where, if
you are new to Seattle, I have alluded to a person or event and
haven't said enough about it for you. Just as, if you have lived
here a long time, there will be information and explanations
you don't need. I hope where I have erred in this respect it is by
giving too much rather than too little, and in order to facilitate
some finding, I have done some cross-referencing in parentheses.

The book starts near where Seattle itself started, on the corner
of First and Yesler, and works out to the city limits in layers.
First, Pioneer Square, downtown, First Avenue–Pike Place Market–
Waterfront, Denny Regrade; second, Seattle Center and lower
Queen Anne, Chinatown/International District, Queen Anne Hill,
Capitol Hill (what might be called the inner ring); then, further
from downtown, along the north shore of Lake Union, past the
University of Washington, down the west shore of Lake Wash-

ington to Seward Park; finally, at the extremities, West Seattle, Magnolia, North End.

Omissions are of five kinds. First are private clubs and residential enclaves, some churches and theaters, any place where a visitor cannot gain access without knowing someone special or sitting through a service or a performance. In some cases a description of the exterior has seemed enough. Where access is available but not by means you can easily see, I have given instructions, but please remember that practices and policies can change without notice. Second, I have omitted many places, most notably small neighborhood businesses, that are rightly loved by those who know them well but can be of little interest to a visitor not currently in need of a range-fed chicken or a bag of nails. I have, though, now and then mentioned a place where anyone, in the midst or at the end of a long walk, might be expected to want to eat or drink. Please remember concerning these and all other retail establishments mentioned by name that nothing disappears more suddenly and often inexplicably than a store, restaurant, or pub; in the couple of years between the writing and publishing of this book a distressing number of beloved landmarks have gone. Third, though I am quite willing to offer negative judgments, I have omitted a good deal that I find uninteresting or even positively offensive. Most of these fall into one of two overlapping categories: large institutional buildings like hospitals, schools, and governmental offices, and buildings built between 1945 and 1965 when large buildings tended to be all glass or else windowless, and houses were suburban ranch or split level. Since tastes do differ, I hope this mention here will give fair warning; I am not one who takes great interest in the labor of the negative unless some point or truth or enlightening comparison is thereby made possible. The fourth kind of omission is the result of my not being able to devise a good walk when all I had to mention was a place or two. I have, but as a kind of sport, included a potpourri last chapter called "Here and There," but it only begins to mention interesting isolated places.

The fifth kind of omission is that which I have never seen or, worse, have overlooked carelessly. The best way you can forgive me is to let me know what I've missed.

I have adapted the following description from *Seattle Past to Present.*

Seattle is slightly above 47° 30′ north latitude, slightly west of longitude 122° west. It is almost due north of Portland and San Francisco, and due west of Great Falls, Montana; St. John's, Newfoundland; Basel, Switzerland; and Budapest, Hungary. A position that far north yields sixteen hours of daylight in June, sixteen hours of darkness in December. The chief determining factor for the climate is not its latitude, however, but its proximity to the Pacific Ocean. A hundred miles west of Seattle, along the coast, is the wettest spot in the continental United States. At Quillayute the average annual rainfall is about 150 inches. Between there and Seattle rise the Olympic Mountains, which absorb much of the moisture coming off the ocean, so that Seattle's annual rainfall averages about 35 inches. The marine air also moderates the temperature: the thermometer has rarely gone as low as zero or as high as one hundred Fahrenheit. When the weather reaches what are for Seattle its extremes, above the low seventies and below the midthirties, it is almost always governed by high-pressure systems inland, and so is dry. The climate is often compared to that of southern England, but Seattle's is much less humid in hot weather.

It is said to "rain a lot" in Seattle, a statement both true and misleading. Its annual precipitation is less than that of all major eastern seaboard cities, none of them famous for rain. The difference: Seattle gets little of its precipitation in the form of snow and even less in the form of heavy thunderstorms. A steady day-long rain in Seattle will make everything seem very wet, while the precipitation may measure only half an inch. It is really wet only in the winter; and in many years, November, December, and January account for almost half the annual rainfall. Between May and October will be two- and three-week stretches with no rain at all.

What does distinguish the climate is the general cloudiness. From late fall through early spring the sun is a relative stranger, and even during dry spells a push of marine air can bring low clouds in at night which last through the morning. Sunrises are more infrequent than sunsets. Winter is short: Thanksgiving to early February. Fall and spring are long and lovely. Summer is California come north: brief, brilliant, cloudless.

It is a magnificent climate for growing things. The great native trees are Douglas fir and hemlock. Before white folks came, the land was covered with these tall and superbly straight trees, mixed with other conifers, half a dozen deciduous trees, and some evergreen shrubs. Compared with the inland valleys of California, the growing season is quite short, but compared with most of the rest of the country, it is long. Since winters are seldom severe and the summers seldom hot enough to leach the soil, evergreen shrubs and trees, rhododendrons, azaleas, camellias, and fuschias are in their element. Gardening is easy, and almost everyone grows something.

The city is bounded by and dotted with bodies of water. On the west is Puget Sound, an inland saltwater sea that leads out through the Strait of Juan de Fuca to the Pacific. This waterway provided the major means of transportation to and from Seattle until the coming of the railroads, and since Seattle is the continental U.S. city closest to Japan and Alaska, it still provides major ballast to the city's economy. On the east is twenty-two-mile-long

Lake Washington, a cool and—at present—clean mountain lake at close to sea level. In between the Sound and Lake Washington is Lake Union, and the three are connected by canals, the one to the west involving a lock. These connecting bodies of water, plus Green, Haller, and Bitter lakes in the north end and the Duwamish emptying into the Sound—by way of Elliott Bay—in the south, convey a sense that water is always near. Seattle has more boat owners than any large American city. The boats range from hydroplane racers and ocean-going cruisers to kayaks, canoes, and dinghies, and many are manufactured in Seattle. Probably because the outdoor swimming season is short, there are too few beaches along the two hundred miles of shoreline. Rimming the shores of Lake Union and Portage Bay are colonies of houseboats, ranging from utilitarian boxes to mansions; some of the houseboat "streets" look like Venice.

The land is almost never flat. It moves from sea level to 457 feet on the top of Queen Anne Hill, less than a mile away. Downtown is built on what was once steep hillside rising away from a cliff above the Sound, and it is surrounded by First, Capitol, Queen Anne, and Beacon hills. Other areas are only relatively flatter, and the constant rise and fall of the land means one is never far from a great view of water, mountains, and other parts of the city. In the winter especially, when the leaves are off the deciduous trees, one is constantly aware of space opening out, to anything from a tall tree or hill a short distance away, to Mount Rainier and Mount Baker, about a hundred miles southeast and northeast.

Since the major building material is wood, the city is dominated by single-family frame houses, and Seattle has the largest percentage of homeowners of any major American city. Population density is relatively low. Many newcomers are struck by great mixing in most residential streets—of architectural styles, income levels, and levels of pretension. People who want to know where the "best part of town" is can only be given a multiplicity of answers. There are "good neighborhoods" (the phrase is frequently used as a euphemism) in Magnolia and Seward Park, Laurelhurst, Windermere, Innis Arden, Blue Ridge; there are "good old neighborhoods" on Queen Anne and Capitol hills, along the ridge west of Lake Washington, on the slope north of Lake Union. In all these areas, and occasionally even in the more outlying neighborhoods, one finds houses of great elegance not far from houses of great plainness. There are many fine houses, relatively few mansions. Concurrently, though many people live at or below the poverty level, that does not express itself visually very much. Just as there is no "best part of town," so there is no "worst."

Seattle is a soft city, made up of soft light, hills, water—all conveying a sense that nature is truly accommodating here. There is no day in the year when it is too hot or too cold to work or get around, few when one cannot be outside, walking or gardening, in a boat, playing tennis or golf, fishing.

Seattle's colors are gray and green.

A final word, about safety. In many of these walks, I have noted that this part is best done alone, or in this or that stretch you will be alone. Obviously I have no desire to put anyone at risk, and it is equally obvious that judgments vary widely as to places that are not safe. It seems important to note what streets and neighborhoods are safe at night because there are plenty of people around, and to say that if you are anxious, walk in the daytime and take a companion.

2 Pioneer Square

The great fire of June 6, 1889, which began in a paint and carpentry shop on the corner of First and Madison when a pot of glue boiled over, was the single event that made Seattle—or would be if single events could do such things. At the time, the only transcontinental rail line to Puget Sound was the Northern Pacific's to Tacoma, and that city was enjoying its brief, brave rash of glory. Seattle, though, was much the more economically dense and diverse of the two cities, so when the Great Northern, James J. Hill's St. Paul based line, came to Seattle as it did in 1893, Seattle quickly emerged as the premier city not just of Puget Sound but of the entire Northwest.

After the fire it was clear that what might first seem disaster was really opportunity: clear the rubble, fill in all marshy land, build again, this time using more brick and stone and less wood, this time with an eye to permanence and even elegance. Some time before the fire, lumberman and mill owner Henry Yesler hired Elmer Fisher to design the Pioneer Building, but actual construction did not start until afterwards. Nothing like it had been seen in Seattle before. (Though most of Seattle's prefire buildings were of wood, one that was not and survives is the Drexel Hotel building on the southwest corner of Third and James. There's a world of difference between it and the Pioneer Building.)

This began a building boom that lasted around thirty years. For about half that time most of the new buildings were in the land-fill south of Yesler, the area known ever since as Pioneer Square. After that, full exploitation of the uses of structural steel and the elevator changed the ways, means, heights, and even the uses of buildings, and growth was north and east of First and Yesler. Per-haps the most striking visible difference between the buildings of the two periods is that Pioneer Square is almost all red, and the downtown that was to be knows almost no red.

The Pioneer Square Historic District, which runs roughly south from Yesler to King, east from the waterfront to Second, is the result of a city ordinance of 1970. A great deal of it looked then much as it had seventy years earlier, since the city gradually turned its back on the oldest buildings in its push north and east from Yesler. In its heyday, Pioneer Square was not only Seattle's business district but the tenderloin, with theaters, opera houses, hotels, and brothels. When the banks and law firms and retailers moved away, taking practically all the live entertainment as well, what was left became mostly warehouses and flophouses. When I moved to Seattle in 1962, much of Pioneer Square was derelict, and downtown business people were promoting a ring-road system to keep the retail core competitive with suburban malls. To build the road, much of Pioneer Square would have been demolished and the rest left to collapse.

The road was never built, and one reason is that between the time the idea was proposed and the time it was abandoned, things were stirring in Pioneer Square and soon the need for the Historic District was apparent even to some who a few years ear-lier had given up on the area. Partial credit goes to François and Julia Kissel, who turned the Pittsburgh Lunch into the Brasserie

Pittsbourg and ushered in a new era of eating in Seattle; Peter Cipra's first Labuznik restaurant; landscape architects Jones & Jones; the lobbying group, Allied Arts of Seattle; the city's federally funded Model Cities program; and Victor Steinbrueck, who fought against the ring road and for the ordinance at every turn, and who, with Sid Cohn, did a building survey of the area in the mid-1960s. But the key figures are Richard White, who opened the first art gallery in the area, on Occidental Avenue, and bought and renovated several buildings along with Allen Vance Salsbury, and architect Ralph Anderson, who bought a number of Pioneer Square buildings and brought to the task of renovation a genius that, even with his example to follow, none has matched. His major accomplishments are the Jackson Building (1963), the Globe Hotel (1965), the Pioneer Building (1970–75), the Grand Central Hotel (1971–73), and the Court in the Square (1984–85). As we'll see in the walk, Anderson got more inventive and robust as he went along.

Since many of the Pioneer Square buildings were originally retail businesses at ground level with living spaces above, a natural consequence of renovation has been apartments and condominiums on upper stories and, more recently, a new apartment house built in imitation of the old style. These residences are not low-income housing by any means, nor are their numbers large, but they guarantee the presence of people whose stake in the area is not just a daytime matter. And this is important. A dozen Ralph Andersons could not keep Pioneer Square from being in part what it has always been, a squatting or staying place for people once called Skid Road bums, now called the homeless. Flophouses no longer exist, and their function is served only by missions. Of these the area simply does not have enough, and that has meant that Occidental Park, which ought to stand as a jewel in the city's crown as bright as two other parks of its era, Gas Works and Myrtle Edwards, is a constant point of tension between a Them and an Us as the homeless use it for their squatting and staying.

Pioneer Square is a great mix, as rich and varied as any in Seattle in the last generation. It still has a good deal of unrenovated space, many of its buildings are in receivership, and it probably needs twice as many residents as it now has in order for the tension between merchants, apartment and condo dwellers, and the Occidental Park transients to abate measurably. But its success is demonstrable. It is where you go in Seattle to show how old buildings can be turned to new uses, which is one of the major ways cities become great cities.

Walk: about two hours.
Bus: any going south on First or Second Avenue. Pioneer Square is within the downtown free ride zone, but the Pioneer Square exit in the bus tunnel leaves you up on Third and out of the area of this walk.

The walk starts at Pioneer Square Park in front of the Pioneer Building and ends a little more than a block away at the corner of Second and Yesler. The area has a pleasant sameness to it, so in trying to get a feel for it, whatever suits you is what you should do. There are maybe a dozen places I'd urge you not to miss, plus maybe half that many that stand out as negative examples of various kinds. What Pioneer Square does most is galleries, rugs, cafes, and taverns, many of which have live music at night. But if none of this is for you, there's still plenty to see.

Start "walking" by sitting for fifteen minutes in Pioneer Square Park—a triangular area also called Pioneer Place—where First and Yesler meet. It's never crowded and almost never empty; it frequently has Native Americans watching, or ignoring, the Tlingit

*Pioneer Building: Elmer Fisher (1889) and Ralph Anderson
(1970) making light in Victorian gloom*

totem pole and the Chief Seattle bust. Sitting here can get you used to one of the area's good qualities, namely that people and buildings always seem more important than cars and buses. To the left of the Pioneer Building you may see people gather for the Underground Seattle tour. Don't be tempted to take it. It will show you 1889 plumbing like nothing else can, but almost everyone feels ripped off, perhaps because they were expecting Pompeii, and you may hear someone emerge loudly expressing disappointment.

The Pioneer Building, which the city uses as its datum point to measure altitudes of buildings and streets, is the Historic District's grandest structure, and is also the oldest important building in Seattle. If you learn to call this Romanesque Revival, you'll have something to contrast with the Renaissance Revival of the Jackson Building, further down First Avenue, both being styles that all but disappeared after structural steel and the elevator came in.

It was in the basement of the Pioneer Building that the Kissels created the Brasserie Pittsbourg in 1970. It is probably hard for anyone who was not here at the time to imagine that before then eating out in Seattle was generally either in decent joints or a few places to go in order to dress up and spend money. After the Brasserie opened, Seattle came to have not only more good restaurants than it can decently afford but better supermarkets, delis, wineshops, espresso bars and carts. And after the Brasserie opened, folks really started "discovering" Pioneer Square.

In the same year, 1970, Ralph Anderson began his renovation of the rest of the building, and it offers a splendid introduction to his work. The lobby is lined with Italian marble, which you should look at hard and then go back out to compare its red with those of the sandstone of the exterior, and do your best to bear both in mind as you encounter other reds along the walk. Then back in, to the handsomely restored cage of the elevator, to the top floor. Start down the stairs, stopping long enough on each floor to look at the collection of photographs of other 1890s buildings. Elmer Fisher designed this central space, which is also an atrium , to provide ample light and ventilation; and Anderson, as if learning from it, made light the signature feature in his Pioneer Square remodelings. There is light here strong enough to moderate the heavy gloom of late Victorian buildings without altering their essential character, atmospheric enough that no one seems to move quickly inside one of Anderson's buildings.

Keep this in mind and go across the park to the Mutual Life Building on the northwest corner of First and Yesler. The rehabilitation here was by Olson/Walker, currently probably most famous for their work with Robert Venturi on the interior of the new Seattle Art Museum. All is not lost here—the elevator cars are as good as those across the street—but the lobby is barren, and upstairs nothing is particularly wrong but no opportunity was seized either. Outside, the postmodern coloring of the exterior is both pointless, because the original coloring was good, and wrong, because, having used it, Olson/Walker felt entitled to use it on the exterior of the Olympic Block Building, which they and others designed in 1985, kitty-corner from the Mutual Life. The old Olympic was one of the area's few victims to the wrecking ball, and there was much talk that the new building was working hard to fit in with its century-old surroundings. You who have lived in Seattle long enough to see how well mere contractors have built houses in the older neighborhoods that blend well with their neighbors can look at the new Olympic, then at its neighbors, and tell yourself that architects will be architects. The best the new Olympic can be called is a near miss, and in this case a miss is as good as a mile.

First Avenue South is the heart of the walk. Go slowly, back and forth across the street. Give Olson/Walker better marks for their work on the Maynard Building on the northwest corner of First and Washington; have a look at the pleasantly restored lobby and stairs of the Delmar Building on the northeast corner; then go west on Washington to see Carl Bergmann's fine rehabilitation of the St. Charles Hotel. All this, though, is to keep you asking what you like and don't like in renovations to set you up for the Grand Central Hotel and Arcade, 208–220 First Avenue South, which was a plain transient hotel in the 1890s, gussied up and renamed in 1907. Ralph Anderson reworked it in the early 1970s. It is probably his best known work, and certainly the one that showed the world how rehabilitation of these buildings could be profitable. The high ceilings of prestructural-steel buildings, then a necessity, now an opportunity to adapt, here yield retail businesses at ground level that seem positively cozy at the foot of the arcade that brings in light from a height of seventy-odd feet. Once again, the soft light is a positive deterrent to any human impulse to make noise or move quickly.

The Grand Central was redone between 1971 and 1973. Those were also the years of the Pike Place Market vote, Occidental Park, Starbucks coffee, Gas Works Park, and our next stop, Elliott Bay Book Company on the southeast corner of First and Main, in the Globe Hotel, also Romanesque Revival and another Anderson project. The skyscrapers downtown are the most obvious signs of change from 1968 to 1990, but seldom the best or most interesting. Those who have lived during this era in Seattle could do worse than stand in Anderson's Grand Central and make a list of changes—bad as well as good if you like—between 1971 and 1973, if your memory is given to pinpoint accuracy, or in the longer stretch beginning in the late 1960s. It's too soon to say just what we have become; what we know is that we'll never again be as we were.

Now on to Elliott Bay Book Company, the biggest single magnet, if you exclude the Kingdome, to the Pioneer Square area. In twenty years it has grown from a single room to a gigantic warren without changing its essential character. The store now has more titles than any bookstore in the Northwest except Powell's in Portland, and it is a mark of its quality that the staff has grown quite large and still is always willing to be helpful and often is surprisingly knowledgeable. Owner Walter Carr is generally in evidence. The rooms yield one to another effortlessly along a diagonal going away from the entrance, and the space is so vast it does not feel claustrophobic even the Saturday before Christmas. In the basement, at the foot of a fine spiral staircase, is the cafe, a roomful of books and daily newspapers for browsing, plus food and drink that is good but naggingly expensive. In the other half of the basement, Rick Simonson hosts readings—as many as seven or eight a week—by authors ranging from the world famous Toni Morrison or Norman Mailer to locals just getting started or established. People in all branches of writing and publishing know Seattle because they know Elliott Bay Books. No book, no teacher, no other institution has done as much to make Seattle more literate, informed, and alive to the possibilities of literary excellence. It's hard just to go in, find and buy a book, and leave.

By now you'll have a feel for upscale Pioneer Square. Cross the street to the Bread of Life Mission to see why it remains important that what once were called flophouses and soup kitchens remain here in the missions. By day you can see the homeless congregating in groups of two or three, pushing their belongings in shopping carts, sleeping on park benches. At night-

Elliott Bay Book Company, one of the great places to browse and buy

fall the edge gets sharper, as the need for shelter grows, along with the various requirements of the addicted. Most Pioneer Square merchants can count customers lost with every homeless they see; most Pioneer Square residents have made their peace with the homeless or they would not live here; the people in the missions go at least one step further and see themselves as advocates of homeless people. If you can, here at Bread of Life or some other mission, you might well stop and give some thought to who in their minds is Them, who is Us, and why.

Next come three striking examples of what not to do and how not to do it. On the southeast corner of First and Jackson is the Heritage Building, where Seattle's largest architectural firm, NBBJ (Naramore, Bain, Brady & Johanson), has its offices. Here is a lobby and staircase that Anderson could have done wonders with, but these guys, having left pipes exposed to show they know how to keep the old, made and painted the staircase to the inner sanctum—no admittance except on official business —as though they wanted to look like a law firm in a downtown skyscraper.

The same thing happens at Merrill Place, across First, between Jackson and King, partly NBBJ work, partly Olson/Walker. You walk into the lobby and instantly feel you don't belong, and someone will be along soon to tell you so. Here, then, the real shock is to exit this space and go into Il Terrazzo Carmine. Suddenly you're in a huge and wonderful room, one of the best restaurant spaces in Seattle, with an exposed kitchen that does not shout its presence, and windows to the west looking onto *il terrazzo* in the warm months and covered by a beautiful curtain in the darker times. Anything but the idea of either NBBJ or Olson/Walker.

If you think I've been too hard on these chaps, leave Merrill Place and walk down First to King and turn left, going far enough so you can get a good look at the Kingdome, perhaps the single worst expression of the energetic outpouring of the early 1970s, which I have been heretofore extolling. NBBJ, the presiding architects, ensured that the building would be brutal and ugly. To see that a massive, free-standing stadium need be nothing like this terrible—in the bad sense—you can compare it with Husky Stadium on the University of Washington campus, essentially the work of George Wellington Stoddard in the architecturally dark time of 1950. In the case of the Kingdome, NBBJ's contribution is only a tithing of what is wrong. In order to get and keep major league baseball and football, Seattle had to have a stadium. It was a hard sell, since, one perceives, while many people elsewhere thought Seattle off the end of the earth if it did not have major league baseball and football, many locals thought they would not miss what they never had. Those doing the selling, who were (or were like) those who created the World's Fair of 1962, approached their task with something less than the confidence they claimed was a major result of the fair. Feeling that the wind was not quite blowing their way, they asked for too little money in the Forward Thrust bond issue. When that failed to pass, they could not imagine that their best next move was to ask for twice as much. What they managed to get approved the next time around was always going to be a cheap building. Worse still, they ignored the evidence, easily available, that Seattle is generally one of the driest cities in America between April and October, so they thought they had to have a dome. And while there may be justification for a dome in hot, humid Houston, there is none for it in Seattle. Nonetheless, a dome was built, and on the cheap, and inside is perhaps the largest expanse of totally dead air in the world, a place of twilight that keeps threatening to move into total darkness.

Court in the Square, Ralph Anderson's atrium masterpiece

You have now seen the worst that Seattle and this walk have to offer; time will wound all of Seattle's heels but this.

Walk back north along Second toward Jackson, and on your left is the Court in the Square, Ralph Anderson's last Pioneer Square work, which he did with Koch and Duarte in the mid-1980s. Here he takes the alley between two buildings—the alley originally being a railroad right-of-way—and encloses it in a series of glass arches and squares in a design like many Romanesque Revival buildings a century earlier. Instantly, he has his atrium, and windows that faced the alley now have boxes and plants. At ground level, a cafe. The Court in the Square is on the outer edge of the Historic District, and it has little in the way of interesting neighbors, but the court is quietly busy and the rental spaces above seem to be mostly occupied. It was Anderson's last major project, and also his most flamboyant, and should be better known.

One block to the north, on Second, on the northwest corner of Main, is the beautiful Waterfall Garden built to commemorate the site where United Parcel Service began—the design of an eastern firm, Sasaki, Dawson & DeMay. It is a classic example of a good thing in the wrong place. On warm spring and summer days there are people here, especially around lunchtime, but otherwise it is usually deserted. The cafe is closed. Perhaps its delicateness is the wrong kind of pretty for Pioneer Square, but the real problem is that it is an enclosed space that can feel lonely and even dangerous without lots of people around. The much larger Freeway Park uptown has suffered from the same problem and survived, but it is nearer to many more people. The Waterfall Garden is locked at night to keep the homeless out, an edgy response to a difficult problem that might have been foreseen.

The contrast to Waterfall Garden is at hand the moment you walk the block on Main between Second and Occidental. On your left is a handsome tree-lined pedestrian mall, and even if you want to see no more cafes or galleries, you should nod a greeting to the Foster/White Gallery, at 311 Occidental South, which White opened before Ralph Anderson restored his first building. By all means, also peek into the lobby of the Seafirst Bank branch on the southeast corner of Occidental and Main. No rehabilitation here: it has been this way for a century.

Outside again, on your right is Occidental Park, the work of Jones & Jones in 1972, after which they designed the African savanna at Woodland Park Zoo. This was only a parking lot before it became park, cobblestones, and London plane trees. Unsurprisingly, it is the meeting place and preferred outdoor sleeping area for the homeless, and is what everyone means when they talk about "trouble" in Pioneer Square. In the 1970s the Kissels' marvelously designed City Loan Pavilion restaurant protruded into the park, but it could not survive the fact that potential customers did not want to come into the park at night. That space is now empty. During the day, however, Occidental Park is very pleasant. Anderson's Grand Central Arcade also opens onto the park, so you can get coffee and pastry and sit outside and remember some places you may never have been, like Paris.

Not much further to go now. Leave the park on Occidental, continuing north, and you'll soon see one of Seattle's best wall advertisements, a painted ferryboat with "Washington State Ferries" above and "Have Lunch Over Seas" below. The ad people have never been able to improve on that one, though the actual lunch on the ferries has never been good. You are looking at the back of the Interurban Building, the work of John Parkinson. It is a square building, but seen from its front, on the corner of Occidental and Yesler, it forms a great triangle, and if you stare a while at the lion's head at the entrance, the different arched window shapes, the different sizes of the floors, the stone carving

and terra-cotta trim, you'll see the Pioneer Building's only rival for Pioneer Square elegance.

Finally, walk up the street to Second and Yesler to get Seattle's best visual history lesson. At an angle of about ten o'clock is the south side of the Pioneer Building to remind you of where you started this walk. At three o'clock is the flagship of what replaced the Pioneer Square buildings when structural steel and the elevator came in, the L. C. Smith Tower of 1914. Up Second is the Alaska Building of 1904, its exterior stretched like skin on its frame, and across Cherry from the Alaska you can make out part of John Graham's terra-cotta masterpiece, the Dexter Horton Building of 1923, which is not the last great downtown building for the next fifty years, but comes close to it.

The first lesson concerns the relation of these buildings to those behind you in the Historic District. One replaced the other via technological advances, and when that happened there would soon be no new Romanesque or Renaissance Revival buildings. Multiple-use spaces were replaced by office blocks, and after that it was half a century before anyone could rethink the Pioneer Square buildings that by then had become derelict. So the contrast between the buildings in front of you and those behind you is very great, yet both are part of that same burst of energy that began with the 1889 fire and the Pioneer Building and ended with World War I and the Dexter Horton.

To lock that thought into place, look up. Looming over all, not like monsters exactly, but not at all like loving parents either, are the western slab of the First Interstate Center, the playful top of the Washington Mutual Tower, the uppermost flange of the

Looking up at Smith Tower and Columbia Seafirst Center, the tallest buildings in each of Seattle's booms, from Occidental Park, created in 1972 to replace a parking lot

Columbia Tower, all part of the next great burst of energy in the 1970s and 1980s. They're impressive, but here, since you can place them historically, you do not have to accept them on their own terms. Feel free to reply to them that the restoration work in Pioneer Square during the years the skyscrapers were built is at least as interesting and impressive as they are.

So first you distinguish 1890–1900 from 1900–1920, and then you lump these together to contrast with 1970–90. Now lump them all together: among the feelings that went into the creation of every one of these buildings were greed, pride, and vanity. Thus considered, *Plus ça change, plus c'est la même chose.* Contemporary greed, pride, and vanity, however, are quite capable of taking care of themselves, while those of the past are not. Pioneer Square could be restored and recreated because it was abandoned, not demolished. No such benign fate met many buildings, on Second Avenue especially, that were too close to where downtown wanted to express itself to survive the last couple of decades. Those that are left—like the Smith Tower, the Alaska and Dexter Horton buildings—need our care and protection. Unfortunately, their spaces are nothing like as adaptable as those Ralph Anderson worked on, so it will take a genius as great or greater to find new uses for them when they become endangered.

Here on this corner is as close as you can come in this young provincial city to the musings of Gibbon amid the ruins of the Roman Capitol in 1764.

Pioneer Square has a reputation for being dangerous, especially for women, women alone, and at night. There are certainly safer places in Seattle at night, but a list of them would also exclude many places covered by the walks in this book, like downtown, the Arboretum, or Seward Park. The point about Pioneer Square, though, is that there are reasons to be there at night, as there are not in much of Seattle. There are the venerable taverns, the Central and the J&M, which date from before any restoration. There are jazz spots, there are the restaurants near First and Jackson, and Elliott Bay Books is open well into the evening.

I have talked to a number of single women who work and live in Pioneer Square, and their testimony is unanimous: if, at night, you stay away from Occidental Park and the waterfront, they feel you are quite safe. One woman who waits tables at the New Orleans, and so does not leave work until midnight, says she feels quite secure walking a few blocks on First to her apartment because along the way there is someone, in every place still open, keeping an eye out for trouble.

No, they say, the real problem with living in Pioneer Square is that there's no good neighborhood market, no place you can buy a spool of thread or a bucket of paint. Actually, you don't have to go much farther here to find these things than you do in most of the post–World War II residential areas of the city, but it feels as though you do because here you'd like to be able to get along without a car and there you know you can't.

3 Downtown

I t does not have ancient walls, like the City of London, or the universally understood boundaries of midtown Manhattan or the Loop. If one is at some distance from it, "downtown" can include anything from the Space Needle to the Kingdome; closer up, "downtown" is between the water and the Interstate-5 freeway, Yesler and Stewart. This walk narrows that still more, and uses Second through Seventh for its north-south streets—leaving First, the Pike Place Market, and the waterfront for the next chapter.

One block north from Yesler and south from Stewart are twelve streets whose names can be remembered as follows: Jesus (Jefferson and James) Christ (Cherry and Columbia) Made (Marion and Madison) Seattle (Spring and Seneca) Under (University and Union) Protest (Pike and Pine).

(For a perspective on early downtown, see Chapter 2.)

Second Avenue became downtown's main street around 1910, after Seattle had tripled its population in the previous decade and the city limits had expanded to where they remained until after World War II. There were the great office blocks, like the

Hoge, the Alaska, and Smith Tower. There were the banks, a few of which remain. There were the department stores: Frederick, Nelson and Munro; the Bon Marché; J. A. Baillargeon; J. S. Graham; Rhodes; MacDougall and Southwick; J. C. Penney—all of which are gone from here. The movement away from Second began during its heyday when Frederick's opened its new store in 1918 way out, north of Pine, between Fifth and Sixth. A dozen years later the Bon moved to its present location between Third and Fourth, and after World War II, though lower Second remained home for banks and major law firms for a generation, the department stores moved or closed. Penney's was the last to go, in the 1970s. Second became a neglected street of faded charm until the skyscraper boom doomed many of its finest old buildings.

When Second Avenue was being developed, government buildings and their satellites began to appear up the hill from Second and north of Yesler, and their successors are still there. But unless you have business there or have been arrested, there is not a reason in the world to pay this area any attention. All one can say is that Seattle is not the only city where the public buildings are among the worst.

A third major feature downtown is the University of Washington's Metropolitan Tract, ten acres bounded roughly by Fourth and Sixth, Spring and Union. This is land that pioneer Arthur Denny, whose original claim covered most of what is now downtown, gave when Seattle gained the right to the territorial university in 1860 provided it could open its doors in a year. A building was built, the University began, though it had no college-level students and was mostly a high school for a generation. In the 1890s, when it was becoming a university for real, it moved to its present location north of Portage Bay. It retained ownership of the downtown tract and watched it become prime property. Office blocks were built along Fourth in the teens, and, in the 1920s, the tract's jewels: the Olympic Hotel, the Skinner Building, the Fifth Avenue Theatre.

In the recent boom, the first skyscraper was the Seafirst, now called the 1001 Fourth Avenue Building. Then came about twenty more, peppering the land between Second and the freeway, between Cherry and Union. The story is told of a family making its first trip to the Grand Canyon, and after everyone had gaped, the youngest says, "What the hell happened here?" Anyone who left Seattle in the 1960s and returned today might well ask the same. An awful lot of "Me too" happened, and an awful lot of "Anything you can do." That is the way with booms. While one of them is going on, there is a great rush to compete. For a while it looked as though there might be at least one bank that did not insist on having its own skyscraper, but the holdout, Seattle Trust and Savings, was sold, and up went the Key Tower. After the banks came the hotel chains, the phone companies, and Martin Selig, local Darth Vader developer, asking "Can you top this?" with the Columbia Tower. Neither the 1986 tax code nor the 1990 CAP initiative, designed to limit the height of buildings, could do more than slow it down. It stopped only when there was an obvious glut, new office spaces remaining unoccupied.

It could have been worse. Individually considered, most of these new skyscrapers are better than the glass slabs built in the 1950s, but those were mostly government buildings put up here and there, and they did not develop any giant vortex of activity. The skyscrapers have permanently altered not just the way down-town looks but what it does. Any area as much given over to a single activity—in this case, offices—must pay the price for being monocultural. In canyonland, restaurants that are packed

Canyonland, from the Smith Tower

for lunch are almost empty for dinner. There are two churches, two movie complexes, only sporadic live theater; that and the new Seattle Art Museum and corporate paintings and sculptures represent "the arts." There are an enormous number of parking spaces, but never enough, and even now that the bus tunnel is finished the streets at rush hour can be so clogged with buses as to be menacing to anyone on foot.

The question of "What the hell happened here?" yields another: "What in all this is distinctly Seattle?" It may be too soon to tell. The lamentations when Frederick and Nelson declared bankruptcy in 1992 were genuine. The downtown store, with its white glazed tile, was distinctly Seattle, so too the Frango mints which Frederick's made and sold exclusively. We need to ask if the second downtown building boom has left us anything as distinctly characteristic as some of the first.

Our Pioneer Square walk ended at Second and Yesler, and our downtown walk must begin there, to glimpse it in its first years of glory, when its main architectural feature was terra-cotta façades and decorations. We begin, and end, in terra cotta. In between is canyonland.

Walk: about three hours.
Bus: any southbound on Second Avenue.

Standing at Second and Yesler, it is easy to marvel at terra cotta's various uses: facing and cornices on Smith Tower, paneling and entrance ornamentation on the Alaska and Hoge buildings, white glazed tile covering the south and west façades of the Dexter Horton. Terra cotta—"cooked earth" in Italian—is any material that has been molded and fired. It quite naturally accompanied structural steel and the elevator in the middle of the first boom because it is fireproof, half the weight of most stone, and, when glazed, keeps moisture out. Terra cotta could not accompany the severer styles of the modern skyscraper. It's too decorative, lending itself to eclectic and therefore suspect styles. Allied Arts of Seattle's *Impressions of Imagination: Terra-Cotta Seattle* is an excellent companion for a downtown walk.

For fifty years the Smith Tower was one of the most distinctive sights in Seattle, by far its tallest building, its tower an index finger pointed to the sky. Now it is dwarfed, not just because buildings on higher ground have more stories, but also because they are meant to be massive, as it is not. Rather than attempt to find a spot to see it as it once could be seen, go inside, press the button for Tower Tickets, and someone will come, ask for a few bucks, and give you a ride to the top; this seems to be the only place on the West Coast where elevators are operated by people. Like all downtown views, that to the west here is spectacular, and you also have the best of Pioneer Square, the International District, and the industrial tideflats. (For a list of views from the top of skyscrapers, see the neat section in Theresa Morrow's *Seattle Survival Guide.*)

Of the other three splendid buildings on Second that you see as you leave the Smith Tower, the Alaska and Hoge are perhaps most distinctive for the way the brick on their upper stories seems like skin stretched taut to the frame. The third, the Dexter Horton, is one of my favorite downtown buildings. It was designed by John Graham, Sr., who did both Frederick's and the Bon, as well as the Key Bank branch (formerly the Savings Bank of Puget Sound) and the Exchange Building farther up Second, and the Joshua Green on Fourth. He is notable not so much for a style as a feel for styles. Here, given half a city block to work with, Graham wanted something impressive. Dexter Horton was Seattle's first banker, and his successors wanted a flagship bank and headquarters. The building has three massive gray marble columns in front, not as entrance but as an announcement of the size of the lobby inside (it is now much lower and smaller). The rest is dressed in white tile terra cotta, spread over so many surfaces. (Be sure to go up Cherry to see the recessed wells Graham used to bring light and airiness inside.) It feels extravagant as well as simple, expensive as well as useful. The ornamentation over the entrance is, like most of Graham's, subdued. For a contrast you might walk a block up Cherry to Third and see A. Warren Gould's marvelous walruses on the Arctic Building. Inside, well, you're in an office building, and the entrance lobby isn't much since the adjacent bank lobby was meant to catch the attention.

The Dexter Horton Bank eventually became Seafirst, which left this building when it built the first of the recent skyscrapers in the late 1960s. As the rush for new giants accelerated, more and more firms moved away from Second Avenue, leaving the older buildings with fewer tenants and less revenue at a time when the boom was also escalating the value of the land itself. Since office blocks, new or old, are much less adaptable to different uses than the older high-ceilinged Pioneer Square buildings, they become at risk easily when newer ones lure office users to what is newest, brightest, ostensibly best. The older buildings can be "saved" by designating them historic landmarks, but that does not make new uses or get new tenants. The city moved offices into the Dexter Horton, as it had earlier into the Arctic Building, as Metro has in various older buildings. This helps a great deal, but the situation remains precarious. More on this later.

Continue north on Second, noting how two of John Graham's other buildings, the Key Bank branch (Bank of Puget Sound building) and the Exchange on the west side, one classical and the other art deco, look awkward side by side. Go into the lobby of the Exchange to see the curved bank of elevators that makes

Lobby and elevators in John Graham's Exchange Building

everyone else's seem boring. Then keep on up Second until you get almost to the corner of Madison.

Most good authorities will declare that canyonland Seattle is best seen properly from (1) a ferry coming into dock at nightfall; (2) Duwamish Head; (3) Gas Works Park on the north shore of Lake Union. All true, but what we're looking for now is views of it from within, and Second and Madison offers an interesting object lesson. From here looking up Madison, you see, as you consider each building one by one, some of downtown's worst. The Key Tower on your left is so blankly brutal it makes the First Interstate, on your immediate right, seem better than it is. The green thing up on Third is the City Light Building, one of Bindon and Wright's 1950s glass slabs. They also took part in the Norton Building behind you on Second at Columbia, and Seattle Public Library's downtown library up on Fourth. Above it is 1001 Fourth Avenue, the characteristically bleak work of NBBJ. You'll have a chance to see for yourself later on why the plaza of 1001 Fourth is the worst place to be downtown, especially on a cold or windy day. Here it is depressing, in need of the lesson taught by Martin Selig's buildings: if you are going to do black in Seattle's gray climate, it had better be shiny and flashy.

None of these buildings could think of anything to be except large, and the City Light is also garish. Yet this is a good view. I doubt that David McKinley once thought of the view looking uphill when he designed the setback to the First Interstate, but the setback is what creates the view, and it is the view that places these buildings as part of a single scene. We will see something similar later when we walk through residential streets on the Lake Washington ridge—houses stacked on top of houses. In both places some individually awful things are taken into a setting and almost transformed.

To show what happens when this placing isn't available in

canyonland, you need go no further than up the hill to the Third Avenue side of the First Interstate and feel that the Columbia Tower and the AT&T Gateway are about to fall on top of you. Flee from this possibility by crossing to the Central Building, handsome gray terra cotta, the last you'll see for a while. If you are of an age, or an inclination, to catch the reference, you might go in to the Central, to Room 440, and find out what business Spade and Archer are in. Outside, you have one more block to climb, up Madison to Fourth, and your climbing is done for the day.

Turn right, far enough past the Fourth and Madison corner to have a good look at the Rainier Club; it's unmarked but I don't think you'll miss it. It is the only downtown building designed by Kirtland Cutter (in 1904). Bebb & Gould added a wing in 1929, so seamlessly it is not easy to see where the seam is. No matter, really, if it is or isn't a handsome building, since it is so obviously one of a kind, takes us back toward another time, and used to have all the ivy and still has much of the lawn downtown. It seems appropriate that this was established as an exclusive men's club (women are now accepted), since greed, pride, and vanity are as evident here as in the huge neighbors surrounding it, the difference being that the Rainier Club is on a scale that make these seem like amiable vices.

Bear in mind this matter of scale as you walk north on Fourth, noting first the aforementioned plaza of the 1001 Fourth Avenue Building, then continue on to the corner of Seneca. What I want you to see is best seen standing in the middle of Fourth here, but since you had better not do that, go into the Four Seasons Olympic Hotel on your right, climb stairs until you find the skybridge to the Unigard Financial Center, and stand in the middle of that. My claim is that this is the most urban view in Seattle, even though none of the buildings you can see are very tall. Partly it is like being on the brow of the hill and looking down

Looking north up Fourth Avenue: Seattle's most urban view, with no skyscrapers

the incline, the traffic moving away from you, pulling the eye along. Partly it is having retail business at street level—something you have seen only intermittently on the walk thus far—which means more people in the sidewalks. Partly it is the billboard at the far end, which encloses the space and makes you notice things like the façade of John Graham's Bon and Carroll's Fine Jewelry street clock. There is no need to fuss the designation "most urban" as long as it can be agreed that it is not necessary to build up fifty stories to gain a striking city effect.

If you want to break the walk in two, or just stop, this is the place. Go back into the Olympic, have coffee in the lobby, a drink or high tea in the Garden Court, or even a meal in the Georgian Room if you have remembered to bring money. These were elegant spaces when George Post and Company, helped by the elegant locals Bebb and Gould, designed them in the 1920s. When NBBJ was chosen to do the rehabilitation in the 1980s, they must have realized that one move toward Mies van der Rohe and sterility and they would be fired, so they entered right into the older spirit. You may feel you are underdressed if you are in casual walking clothes, but many hotel guests arrive and leave wearing shorts, sweats, and sneakers. You will soon feel convinced, also, without having to make the actual comparisons, that this is the finest hotel space, perhaps the finest interior space, in downtown Seattle—the buzz of talk but no sense of noise, movement but no feeling of hurry or crowd, the employees all off to the side and neither knowing nor caring if you find a bathroom or do not spend a dime. As little as ten minutes here can restore body and soul, and set you up for the remainder of the journey.

Leave by the Seneca Street entrance, turn left, cross Fifth and then Sixth and go into Freeway Park. Lawrence Halprin is the architect of record, Angela Danadjieva did the design, Edward Macleod the landscaping, and, since these are mostly San Francisco people, thanks to whoever thought to hire them. The park is a long series of steps and sections extending all the way up to the Convention Center on Pike; best is near the southern end of the park, which has a George Tsutakawa fountain, the most sun, the most lavish planting, the most people. Like many downtown places, Freeway Park is primarily a weekday, daytime affair; it can feel eerie on a nippy Saturday afternoon when you may be the only person awake in it. One of the nicest features of having so many steps and sections is that, though they create or contribute to the eeriness, when the park is crowded it can still feel private. About halfway through, you'll actually be over the freeway, and you will find a waterfall that does an amazing job of masking car noise. A little further on you'll see in the distance the green of the side of the Convention Center, which is of a hue both quite like and a light year from that of the City Light building I made you look at from Second and Madison. The green here is deeper, like that of nearby trees and shrubs, and the plantings also work to keep this from seeming a bare slab.

More impressive, though, than anything about the Convention Center, which if you explore it will seem most remarkable for its adroit handling of traffic flow problems, is the enormous building that dominates the sky from the middle of Freeway Park on. It is Two Union Square, the first of the blue-green "postmodern" buildings we have encountered, though the last to be built. You have seen 1001 Fourth Avenue, and the Unigard Financial Center. You may also know the Public Safety Building, or the Health Sciences Building at the University of Washington. In which case you will be pardoned for not recognizing Two Union Square as the work of NBBJ. The imp was let out of the bottle here. Perhaps it was the great public interest taken in the Washington Mutual Tower,

Two Union Square, sheets of building rising up

the first of the blue-green buildings. Perhaps it was the utter sterility of the adjacent One Union Square, which NBBJ did not design but might once have done. Whatever, this is the one NBBJ building that shows signs of having been fun to design: sides of unequal widths, sides of different curves and bulges, so a complete circuit is necessary to take in all its ripples, plays of light. Also good is the three-story courtyard, which is really a continuation of Freeway Park, and it too is dominated by a waterfall. You can sit outside here on all but the nastiest days, and it is especially nice for those who *like* the feel of canyonland—huge sheets of building rising up.

Out of the courtyard and onto Union, for a moment you are back in terra-cotta Seattle, facing the Eagles Auditorium, the design of Henry Bittman, who was also responsible for the Terminal Sales Building at First and Virginia, also a work of straightforward shape and decorative exuberance. It is derelict. Before Union Square and the Convention Center went up, it was tucked away for few to see, but now hundreds of conventioneers pass it every day, and it must be hoped someone can think of what to do with it. Recent nearby development has sent the value of the land soaring, so that what might be an ideal tenant—like the Cornish School, which could use it as a conservatory and performance hall—cannot possibly afford it. There was talk of using it as a grand public space for an adjacent new hotel. Whatever. Three of downtown Seattle's finest older buildings— the Eagles, the Coliseum Theater, and Frederick and Nelson— now stand empty. There are plans: a shoe manufacturer moving into the Coliseum, Banana Republic moving into the Coliseum, Nordstrom's taking over the Frederick's building, ACT (A Contemporary Theatre) moving from lower Queen Anne to the Eagles. All three buildings have been designated historical landmarks, but that creates no new use for them. The point might be made thus: amid the skyscraper boom and the office glut, and, no question, partly because of it, certain things happened downtown, good things, inventive things, accommodating things, that had not been thought of, or were not thought possible, in earlier years. However one assesses downtown's last generation, it could cap its achievement by reworking these three terra-cotta beauties to some bona fide new use.

Down Union to Sixth and into City Centre Shops, which is gray marble at the base of U.S. Bank Centre, the most upscale of the postmodern blue-greens, the work of the Callison Partnership. I am no fan of the gray marble, and I would not know how to buy anything in these shops, but the space is great fun to walk around in, and to realize how far skyscraper developers and architects have come from the deadly street level spaces at 1001 Fourth Avenue and the Bank of California (also at Fourth and Madison). From the upstairs lobby on Pike, you have a view of the Coliseum, the major remaining B. Marcus Priteca movie theater and one of his few remaining buildings. The most active thing on this corner is the espresso cart in front of Nordstrom's. Look at the cart, and the crowd that is often around it though others are mere yards away. Remind yourself to tell the next person you hear lament the excesses of canyonland that before the skyscrapers, street vending and consuming were illegal in Seattle.

Leave U.S. Bank Centre on the opposite side from the one you came in. If you are doing this walk at a single shot and took no break at the Olympic, you may be tired and in need of skipping the next two segments. In that case, walk through Nordstrom's kitty-corner and come out onto Westlake Park.

But if you have time and energy left, walk south on Fifth, long known as downtown's most elegant street. Though individual shops change here all the time, the tone manages to stay the same. Partly it is the Norway maples lining both sides of the street. Partly it is the Skinner Building, on your left between Union and University. Elegant though terra cotta looks on many older buildings, equally elegant is the unadorned sandstone of the Skinner, the design of R. C. Reamer. The simplicity of this façade lets and even forces the shops themselves to make the statement. Within this building there is also the Fifth Avenue Theatre, which houses traveling Broadway shows and other glitzy events sporadically throughout the year. (You can call to arrange for a tour.) It is the major obvious rival of the Four Seasons Olympic Hotel for the title of downtown's best interior space. Since the Music Box was demolished and the Coliseum closed, this and the Paramount are all that remain of the Prohibition era's love of the movies.

Across Fifth from the theater is Minoru Yamasaki's attempt to make verticality seem attractive; there certainly have been worse attempts, some nearby. Near the base of the tower you will see a sign directing you up to Rainier Square Park, which is on the other side of the tower and faces onto Fourth and University. For some reason it is little known. Granted, it looks out on a much less exciting scene than from the skybridge just up the street, because you are facing the Olympic, which is more attractive inside than out, and some other ugly buildings you cannot see from the skybridge. Still, it is a good place from which to see terra-cotta decoration on the buildings opposite. The quiet here may lead you to discover one of downtown's best kept secrets: except during rush hour, traffic in downtown proper is seldom heavy. This park needs no waterfall.

Now you are back on Fourth, going north. One of the most charming older buildings, the White-Henry-Stuart, was demolished to build what is now the Security Pacific Bank Tower, but much good remains—the Cobb, the Joshua Green, the 1411 Fourth Avenue, the Fourth and Pike, the work of Graham and Reamer among others.

North of Pike is Westlake Park, and at the far end, Westlake Center. This large space was the subject of much hue and cry during the recent skyscraper boom, because here was a "chance"—perhaps a "last chance"—to do something other than go tall. When the task was left to the Rouse Corporation of Baltimore, it was understood the result would be gaudy, which it is, and off-putting, which at least the façade of Westlake Center is. It is always jarring to see such tackiness between the Bon and Frederick's. Downtown needs this, however. If you take stock of some of the stores you have seen in the last hour—like Gucci, Abercrombie and Fitch, Burberry's, Joan and David, Butch Blum, Brooks Brothers—you will probably realize why Westlake had to be as it is: potato chips and fries and Diet Coke because not everyone wants a latte and a salad of assorted greens. A good deal of the time, but especially on Saturdays when much of downtown is dozy and the office workers are at the Wallingford Center or on the golf course or riding a ferry, Westlake is alive, the shops crowded, tables and benches full. Especially if a steel drum band is playing, you can hang out happily for an hour without a book or a newspaper, just looking and listening. The people here also ride the monorail, and make Seattle Center a success, too, as something other than high culture on Mercer. Nice weekdays you can see that half the teenagers in the county are skipping school. So Westlake may be all wrong in theory, but it is dead right in practice.

At the far end of this most urban space, on Fourth where Olive splits off from Stewart, is a street corner that ought to be one of Seattle's finest because the separate elements are so good. First,

there is the Bon, downtown's best gray-tan building, and it is worth riding up and down the escalators inside just to see all the different floor tiles. Across the street is the Mayflower Park Hotel, which has an elegant bar. Between Olive and Stewart, the tri-angular Times Square Building (Bebb & Gould), across Stewart the Centennial Building (Henry Bittman), and across from the Bon, the Securities Building (John Graham). The problem with this corner is the opposite of that at Second and Madison. There the buildings are awful, but the view shapes and tames them. Here the buildings are fine, but there is no place from which to see them. The motor-to-foot-traffic ratio is bad, and the Darth Vader building itself—the Fourth and Blanchard—leers at you from up on Fourth. Do the best you can with this one, then head west on Stewart to Third and face left (south).

Third is not what it once was, but it is closer to it than any other of the north-south arterials. It has Woolworth's, it has buses going both ways so it is always crowded, it has low-rise buildings of little distinction that have managed to dodge the wrecking ball, and it has a newsstand on the southeast corner of Pike where, day or night, you can buy the *Racing Form* and other things besides *USA Today*.

It also has, and you are looking right at it, the Washington Mutual Tower—the first of the blue-green skyscrapers of the late 1980s, designed by the New York firm of Kohn-Pederson-Fox along with McKinley/Gordon locally. My guess is that this color, and the slightly wacky designs it seems to have encouraged, will eventually be a downtown signature as much as white glazed tile is. In that case the Washington Mutual Tower will come to seem as important as the Smith Tower was for so long. Let it be noted that it does not matter if the Washington Mutual Tower is a clone

Westlake Center, all wrong in theory, but dead right in practice

of a building in New York, any more than it matters if the New York Trade Center is a clone of Yamasaki's Security Pacific Tower; the point is only what happens to a building in a particular place.

In this case, the particular space matters a lot. It stands at the northwest edge of the new skyscrapers, and from many angles throughout the city, as far away as East Cherry in Madrona or Corliss North in Wallingford, it is the outstanding downtown building. From other angles, where you can see the Columbia Tower and the AT&T Gateway as well, they do not dominate just because they are taller, and only feel like background to this more massive and striking building. It is currently splendidly framed from down on Western Avenue because of the hole in the ground between Western and First. You can also play peekaboo with this one—from rather distant spots on the waterfront, from an alley between Second and Third down near the Dexter Horton, from the Fifth Avenue entrance to Frederick's. Who would want to do that with the Fifth and Marion Building, or the First Interstate? But it is, alas, dead at street level.

"Postmodern" is perhaps the least expressive name for a style that we have. Even "neoclassic" says more. There is reason for this, since "postmodern" would not exist except that "modern" preceded it. In this case, the Washington Mutual Tower exists because for twenty years one boring modern skyscraper after another went up in downtown Seattle. Kohn-Pederson-Fox are like the prodigal son, or any younger sibling who acts up because the older ones are so pure, or righteous, or whatever, as long as it includes boring. The façade of the Washington Mutual Tower, thus, often bears no relation to the rest of the building; it is its own work of art. Form follows function here only occasionally

Washington Mutual Tower, which purists hate and the general public loves

and only as another piece of fun. Purists hate it, and the general public loves it.

Here is a nice irony. It was only with the skyscrapers of the late 1980s, of which the Washington Mutual Tower and its spinoffs are the most prominent examples, that it became clear there was now a glut of offices, and the boom was over. If developers had been more sensible, then, these might never have been built and we'd have to settle for the Columbia Tower as this generation's signature building. This irony, though, only repeats an earlier one, because something very similar happened in the first boom. Seattle's economy had become soft by the end of World War I and the General Strike of 1919. Predictions of future growth never materialized. Buildings kept going up, though, all through the 1920s. These were some of our finest, like the Dexter Horton, the Skinner, the Bon, and others on the northern edge of downtown. So it would seem that very excess can bear some rich fruit. Had there been no Washington Mutual Tower, standing here and looking down Third Avenue you'd have nothing better to see than the 1111 Third Avenue Building, one of the most boring of our skyscrapers, and now almost impossible to see unless you are right next to it.

4 First Avenue
Pike Place Market
Waterfront

A generation ago, Pioneer Square was lying largely un-
used, Pike Place Market was revered but musty and quiet,
and First Avenue was Skid Row, home to the homeless,
sex shops, bookstores loaded with pornography, gun stores, out-
fitters to Alaska, LOANS. The Downtown Association's ring-road
plan would have turned it into parking lots. Then Pioneer Square
rumbled to life, and, as if in response, the downtowners said they
wanted the Market—to "modernize" it. The response was the
Save the Market drive, led by architect Victor Steinbrueck. By
means of an initiative vote in 1971, the Market, if not exactly
"saved," began an exciting new life as a historic district governed
by a public authority.

One would have thought that First Avenue, the natural link
between Pioneer Square and the Market, would follow suit.
Unlike Second, First did not have difficult-to-remodel office
buildings; almost everything was two to six stories high and
structurally sound. As we'll see, good things have happened on
First, especially on the west side, but it has been a step forward, a
step back, another step forward, stall. There's a similar story to be
told about the waterfront, though the opportunities and pitfalls

are different. So this is an area, potentially the most interesting in central Seattle, whose story is very much incomplete.

Walk: two to three hours, plus time spent inside the museum and the aquarium.
Bus: ride free down First to Columbia.

The First Avenue that was built in the years after the 1889 fire was as much serviceable as grand, as can be seen if you compare the Colman Building, on the northwest corner of Columbia, with the Pioneer Building, or the Globe Building, now the Alexis Hotel, with the Maynard or the Schwabacher Building down on First South. Between 1915 and 1975, the only new building was the art deco Old Federal Office Building. The street went to seed and few noticed and few cared.

That may not be so easy to see as you walk up from Columbia—partly because of the upscale shops at ground level in the Colman Building but mostly because of the new Federal Office Building across from the old one. Hundreds of employees and their clients come and go every day, which must give a boost to First Avenue's economy, but nonetheless the relation of building to street is uneasy. It is not architect Fred Bassetti's fault, since he did not pick the site, decide the amount of office space, or even get to have it dressed in brick as he wanted. The money ran out, and he was forced to go to poured concrete. Bassetti tried to harmonize the relation of the new building and the old one opposite, but the result is only a good try. Seen from street level on First, the new building looms, and looming is not what is wanted on a relatively modest street like First. It works splendidly up on Second, but not here.

Past the two federal buildings, on the left is the largest privately sponsored rehabilitation effort in Seattle, the work of Cornerstone Development and the Bumgardner Architects in 1982–83. The renovation is almost completely successful, but for a number of reasons the results have not been as good as they might have been. The most important building in the two blocks between Madison and Seneca is the Alexis Hotel—small, luxurious, and able, especially in its bedrooms, to make most hotels uptown seem like what they are, chain operations. But if you look out from the lobby of the Alexis, across First, you see Warshal's Sporting Goods and Central Gun, in small, old buildings. These are enterprises of a kind that downtown should never lose, but they are only hanging on here, and look especially drab across from a luxury hotel. The renovations here—the Alexis, the Arlington Building, the new and old Watermark Tower, and the National Building down on Western—should have spawned others, but they have not. It probably says something that the Alexis, widely acknowledged as a success, has had many turnovers in its own dining room and the pub/restaurant space on the corner of Madison and Western. These need more than the hotel clientele to support them, and their surroundings just don't supply it.

As for reasons. The visible ones are Warshal's and Central Gun, with the Second and Seneca Building slouching down. But if these don't help much, they probably don't hurt badly. Also, the original buildings here are not as eyecatching as their Pioneer Square contemporaries. The real villain is the two block long, two block deep hole in the ground just north of the Cornerstone project. It has been there a decade, paralyzing everything near it. And since across from the hole are run-down buildings, LOANS and CHECKS CASHED, Cornerstone ends up isolated, its success precarious. What is even sadder, when Harbor Steps, a project long in the works, finally does fill the empty space, it almost certainly will prove to be too large and impressive for First

Avenue. If the pawn and loan shops probably are no longer really important to have on First Avenue, the size of their buildings is.

This brings you to the corner of University, and Seattle's most talked about new building, Robert Venturi's Art Museum. One glance, and then repeated looking, shows a crucial fact: it is the right size and shape building for First Avenue, and having the corner of First and University be its focal point pushes the eyes up both sides, both streets, making it fit into its surroundings.

As for the rest—the colored tiles, stuck like food pieces into rolled out dough, reminiscent of shapes on Northwest Indian totems, the SEATTLE ART MUSEUM lettering at the top looking more like doodles than an announcement, the long ramp inside with yellow flanges hanging from the ceiling, the columns in the lobby that support much less than they could—all this is Venturi at play, being insistently postmodern. Opinion about all this is divided, inevitably. I like the exterior more than the main interior, but am so happy this building is where it is that I don't really fuss what I do or don't like after that. Even the *Hammering Man* metal sculpture out front, which seems very tacky, is better here than it would be in most other parts of downtown.

The museum itself, as distinct from the building, is primarily the work and the inspiration of Richard Fuller, whose money lay behind the building of the first museum in Volunteer Park, and whose elegant taste shaped the museum's collection for almost fifty years. Fuller realized he was getting into the museum game too late for him to assemble much in the way of great European paintings; the Samuel Kress collection on the fourth floor is minor European painting from the Renaissance and after. Fuller bought pieces from the Near East and Asia as well as Pacific Northwest art, both older Native American and modern. Since the museum owns much more than it can show, and since it has little of world-class quality that must always be on display, what is being

Venturi's Seattle Art Museum, with Jonathan Borofsky's Hammering Man *in front*

shown changes frequently. The one work I urge you not to miss is Mark Tobey's *Rummage,* a white-light celebration of Pike Place Market. It may be the finest work of art created in and about Seattle, and it certainly is a splendid introduction to the next segment of this walk.

As you leave the museum and continue north on First Avenue, you will begin to feel yourself inside the by now quite large magnetic field of the Market. You can plunge in by going into the South Arcade, but you'd be better off going on to the corner of First and Pike, where you can pick up a map and the outline of a walking tour at the Information Booth in the street on your left.

Pike Place Market. Farmer's Market. Or just the Market. It officially began in 1907 as an attempt to lower produce prices by bypassing middlemen and having farmers bring their goods to market themselves. Pike Place, then and now, was at the edge of downtown proper, except that "edge" then really was edge, since there was no viaduct then, no Western Avenue climbing the ridge, and the shoreline extended only about to where Alaskan Way is now. Around this generally little-wanted space grew up a warren of sheds and alleys and, in the next decade, buildings on the slope between Pike Place and First.

When I moved to Seattle in 1962, the emphasis was on being suburban rather than urban, and the impression people gave me was that downtown was okay if you liked that sort of thing, and Chinatown and the Market at either end of downtown were nice places too, if you liked that sort of thing. At the time there were fewer permits for farmers being issued than there had been in the fall of 1907. There were fish markets, high stalls for imported produce, a butcher, a baker, and a candlestick maker, but except in summer and on weekends it was a dozy place. Then the downtown people made their threatening gestures to modernize the Market (for which Kirk, Wallace, and McKinley drew up plans), the

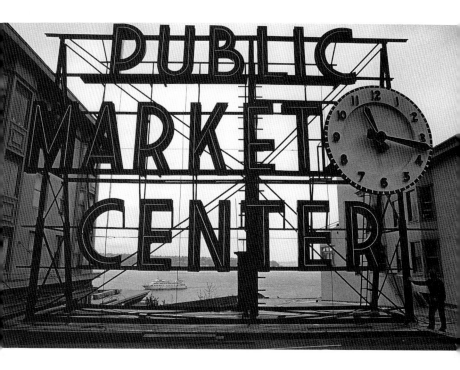

Seattle's landmark sign for more than seventy-five years

public was galvanized into opposition, and within a few years everything changed.

Of all the major changes in Seattle in the years after the late 1960s, those in the Market were among the most important, the most characteristic, and the best. The Market was "saved" by the 1971 initiative and the subsequent creation of a Historic District to be governed by a public Preservation and Development Authority. That meant there were few visual changes as the entire place was renovated by a whole host of local architects, most importantly George Bartholick, and every effort was made not to alter the "character" of the Market. In a city exploding with new energy, though, in which "urban" no longer meant "slum," and "crowd" did not mean "danger," the Market was a place for people, ideas, and money. Gentrification was the result. Out went the liquor store because it attracted winos, down came some rattletrap hotels on First Avenue, in went fancy restaurants, kitchen stores, a new hotel. Victor Steinbrueck, the Market's savior, hated the way it became home for condo dwellers rather than the homeless and the poor, hated its becoming a place for crowds to come and gawk. However, local farmers are still given priority, craftspeople must make whatever they sell, no franchises or chains are allowed, and the Market is a place well worth your making your way through the crowds and gawking.

In one sense, those who are in the Market every day face the same problem as the first-time visitor: on a wintry January day one can move about freely, but there will be few local farmers or craftspeople around; on a lovely July Saturday, the farmers and craftspeople line the tables along the North Arcade and the slabs, the place is full of what it is famous for and does best, but there is gridlock on First Avenue and the place is so crowded it can feel like the floor of Yosemite or the rim of Bryce Canyon on that same July day. Though I am fond of berries picked the morning

I buy them, most of my favorite places—DeLaurenti's Speciality Foods, Pike Place Fish, Frank's Quality Produce, Le Panier (especially for *feuilletée*), and Bavarian Meat Products (especially for braunschweiger)—are open year round, so I avoid the days of thickest crowd. Everyone should see it, though, at least once, at its allest, Thursday through Saturday or Sunday from late spring through early fall.

In another sense, those who know the Market enjoy a huge advantage, because they can find lesser used routes, ignore whatever they don't at the moment care about, lounge with the musicians, or move efficiently toward some desired end. My suggestion if you are a first-time or infrequent visitor is to bring a shopping bag, decide ahead of time on one thing you'd like if you can find it, agree to buy one thing you hadn't expected to want or need, and don't try to do it all.

Scan the map and the walking tour to get your bearings, then move down Pike Street to where it meets Pike Place. Note the sign that says "To Lower Levels and Hillclimb," since that's the way you want to go when you leave. Then make your way along the North Arcade, the heart of the Market. On your right it is local farmers, then high stallers, then locals again, giving way to craftspeople; on your left, fish dealers and butchers, two legendary eateries (Lowell's and the Athenian Inn), some high stallers, a cheese merchant, craftspeople further on. Most craftspeople like to talk about how they make what they make, as do most local farmers who are comfortable speaking English. The high stallers and the fish peddlers tend to be brisker, but also more theatrical; stopping to gawk at them is quite in order.

Across the intersection of Pike Place and Western Avenue is Victor Steinbrueck Park. Since so much of the "new" Market made Steinbrueck nervous, it is appropriate that his park be a little seedy, allow all but the most aggressive panhandling, and permit drunks to sleep unmolested. Even on crowded days you can usually find a niche at the ledge or a spot on the lawn and enjoy the great view of the Sound, rest, discover the meaning of it all.

As you work your way back, now along the east side of Pike Place, you're where the greatest changes have come. No local produce or crafts here; instead a dazzling array of foods and food-related things, cooked, raw, baked, ethnic, hot, alcoholic, day old, a lot of it meant to be eaten as you walk. If this trip is going to involve eating and drinking, sitting down or standing up, this is where to do it; you definitely must ignore all of same down on the waterfront later on. Sitdown places are up the hill or back in the Pike Street arcade; so too are kitchen stores. There'll be a long line at Three Girls Bakery, live crustaceans crawling at Jack's Fish Spot. By now you probably have discovered that the fastest walking is in the street, where the motor traffic moves either slowly or not at all.

Back at the Pike Street/Pike Place junction, your aim is to go down—down to antique shops and collector's items on the lower levels, down to the skybridge over Western Avenue, down the hill-climb that extends to Alaskan Way and the waterfront. Wait for a trolley unless the weather is poor or you are running out of time and energy; the schedule of trolleys is posted, and they come pretty frequently in the warmer months. Your fare is good going in either direction for a couple of hours, giving you time to take the trolley to the end of the line to the north and walk Myrtle Edwards Park to the public fishing pier and back. The park is a joint venture of the city and the Port of Seattle, and is the kind of thing that happens when a city is going well and people don't instantly balk at an idea. I am someone who usually hates to return the way I came, but in this instance going out and returning feel like two different walks. Going out you're most aware of water, breeze, salt smell, the grain elevators, boats, the

Myrtle Edwards Park, going out and coming back

Olympic Mountains if they're visible. Coming back it is buildings in the Regrade, especially Martin Selig's black shiny ones, the panorama of the downtown skyline, the container cargo cranes in the distance, and, for some unknown but real reason, the sky. In Myrtle Edwards you can feel you have left the city without leaving it, left all sense of press and pressure. But this is very much a city park and the joggers here will all be returning to city offices. The total walk is around three miles, and most of the time people feel they have as much energy leaving the park as they did entering it.

The Port of Seattle moved into new offices at Pier 69 early in 1993. Hewitt/Isley did a superb job of renovating the long abandoned American Can Company Building, and if any of the Port's other plans to remake this end of the waterfront are of equal quality, Seattle is in for a treat. The building is long enough to house a prone Space Needle, and while, yes, the main two floors are just a long corridor with offices on either side, that description seems quite inappropriate. What do we find here? A watercourse down the middle of the corridor. All but a few of the offices in cubicles without doors to bring working space into central space. Skylights and big windows facing the water. A generally muted tan-gray broken by splashes of color on some walls. Austere, yes, but never stiff or formal. This instantly became the best governmental building in the city, and by some margin. If you visit during working hours, get someone in Engineering to outline the Port's ongoing plans for this area.

The working waterfront is at either end; the central part has not been a place to load or unload cargo except passengers for a long time. It might be called a tourist trap except that it is not devious enough to constitute a trap. To be sure, no one has ever tried to cook good food in a waterfront eatery, but what you get isn't overpriced, and if the goods in the stores are mostly knick-

Port of Seattle offices, as created from a warehouse by Hewitt/Isley

knacks and souvenirs, they aren't expensive. Most of the people are tourists, of course, and I can never walk here without worrying if the children in these families can find anything to engage their attention.

The main drag is no more than half a mile long, Pier 59 down to Pier 52. Pier 59 is the Seattle Aquarium, designed by Bassetti/ Norton/Metler/Rekevics—the one stop on the waterfront other than the Port's building I think you must make. It is less than twenty years old, and it has grown very nicely in that time. If it is not yet in the class of Tacoma's at Point Defiance, the gap is mostly closed. Indoors the key display is the coral reef, beautifully colored fish, some astonishingly thin, sharks moving at a great rate. The last time I was there, so was an excellently informed young guide. Outside you can touch a crab or a starfish in the Touch Tank, then walk through the small, excellently designed circle called Birds and Shores. The best thing about Salmon and People is its cry of alarm at all that people do to threaten wild salmon. (For actual viewing of salmon you'll do much better at the locks out in Ballard than here.) Inevitably, the *pièces de résistance* are the mammals, sea otters, and harbor seals, better seen underwater than coming up for air, and seen best of all when being fed. It's an hour well spent.

Besides the Aquarium, the other attraction of the waterfront is the variety of boats you can get onto and go someplace: to Victoria, B.C. (Pier 69), the locks (Pier 57), or Tillicum Village on Blake Island (Piers 56 and 55); to sail (Pier 56) or fish (Pier 54); and ferries to Bremerton and Bainbridge Island (Pier 52), and passengers-only service to Bremerton and to Vashon Island from Pier 50. Some of these run year round, some during warm months only.

It took years for the Port to get moving on its Waterfront Plan, but now that it has, we can hope its ambitions—a marine museum, a conference and trade center, a hotel, a short-stay marina—will not just prove another white elephant. Private money has not been pouring in to do its bit, and public money has been best spent in the last generation when the project is no larger than Occidental Park or Myrtle Edwards. The waterfront needs to be something other than a pleasant, tacky place for tourists. Now that both the Port's plans and those for the Harbor Steps project are moving toward reality, this could happen, though the jury may long be out when it comes to judging the results.

For a long time the waterfront was cut off entirely from the rest of downtown. The Market hillclimb built a link, and we need more. And the activity on the waterfront is creating reasons for more. By the turn of the century this could be one of the liveliest areas of Seattle. It could also fall victim of that tendency for planning to get elephantine as it gets ambitious and expensive.

By the time you've reached the ferry terminal at Pier 52, it will be time to turn left and find your car or a First Avenue bus back uptown.

5 Denny Regrade

Probably the only city engineer anyone can remember is R. H. Thomson, and with reason. For over thirty years he envisaged and enacted the works—on the water supply, on the sewage system, on the first hydroelectric power system, on the filling in of the tideflats and the creation of Harbor Island, on the creation of the locks—that still stand as models of their kind. Ironically, though, the work for which he is most remembered was perhaps the least needed and even the most damaging. Seeing with an engineer's eye, Thomson wrote: "I felt Seattle was in a pit, that to get anywhere we would be compelled to climb out if we could." At the south end of central Seattle, Thomson regraded Jackson Street and authorized the sluicing of the north end of Beacon Hill, which made a cut that opened the city up to Rainier Valley and provided the land that filled the tideflats. So far so good, but that left him with an imposing steep hill at the north end of downtown, and between 1899 and 1912 Denny Hill was regraded. Because it was entirely paid for by the owners of the land, those who refused to pay had their land left at its former level, so that for a long time parts of the area looked like an Egyptian desert with pyramids. The very last of the regrading was not done until the time of the World's Fair in the early 1960s.

Thomson's thought, of course, was that downtown would continue to push northward just because, topographically, it could. Not so. Stewart has remained the northern boundary of what most people think of as downtown. Almost twenty years ago, I wrote, "We have what is still called the Regrade, a chronically semi-blighted area, at its best the home for small service industries and a nice faded apartment or two, at its more frequent worst the home of car lots and garish motels and claims that Jesus Saves placed next to cut-rate furniture and clothing stores."

A lot of what I described is still there, often in exactly the form it was then, but the Regrade has changed, changed interestingly, for the better, and in ways that are as much a model for urban vitalization as in its different ways Pioneer Square is. But it is harder to see this in the Regrade, harder to get a feel for what differences the changes make. If it would not be entirely appropriate to say to someone leaving downtown and beginning to walk north, "Look your last on all things lovely," it can be said that little in the area is visually attractive. But that—it turns out—contributes to its vitality, its understated way of being charming.

The less time you have in Seattle, the newer you are to the city, the less need you have of doing this walk. For those who know the city, it is required. It's not long.

Walk: forty-five minutes to an hour.
Bus: no need.

You start at the corner of First and Lenora, within the magnetic field of recent Pike Place Market development. Two large apartment/condo blocks are just behind you, and like all but one of the new residences in the Regrade they aren't much to look at, but they provide the people who are an essential ingredient in changing a neighborhood. Down the street is Continental Plaza, at thirty stories just about the tallest in the city, and Bell Tower, and further down you can see a building that has only five stories, including parking garage, but covers an entire block.

Walking north from Lenora you have one snapshot after another of new/old: Regrade upscale in the Patagonia next to the Army-Navy surplus store that has been there forever; aged resident Continental Furniture giving way to Paisan on First cafe and Darbury Stenderu, so hip it need not tell you what it is. Across Blanchard, the Queen City Grill, laid back and probably as far north as lunchtime office workers go, fit in next to the Frontier Room, the kind of bar that opened in the 1950s when liquor by the drink was first available. Across the street, the strange and interesting Casa-U-Betcha next to oldtimer Consolidated Printing. One reason these mixes are never uneasy is that the apartment blocks all have retail space at street level. Another is that the new upscale stores whisper their presence. Darbury Stenderu is muted in appearance, the Queen City Grill uses a neon sign that has been there longer than it has, Patagonia and Casa-U-Betcha are neatly fit into old, low buildings. The way to be chic here is not to look it, and the Bell Building on the corner may be the oldest in the Regrade and the least chic.

Turn right on Bell. Up a block, on the left, Catholic Community Services has recently turned its bookstore into the Homeless Art Gallery, where current and recent homeless can learn an art or craft. Across from it is the venerable and venerated 211 Club, a pool and billiard hall, larger than the one in the town I grew up in but otherwise identical, the lifestyle anything but smoke free, the air feeling as though Don Dunphy ought still to be calling Friday night fights on the radio here.

You'll have noticed that we are looking at ground-level businesses in the Regrade, as we did relatively seldom in Pioneer Square or downtown. You need to adjust to what there is, and here we are mostly looking at how old relates to new. Thus, on the corner of Third and Bell, you have buildings and businesses that have been here a long time: on the southeast corner, Kelly's Tavern, Mom's Teriyaki, and the small Seville building with a handsome entrance-cum-balcony that manages to squeeze seventeen offices into it somehow; to the northeast, the Adams Apartments. Much more recent is Regrade Park on the southwest corner, and more recent still is Marvin Gardens on the northwest.

Regrade Park is much smaller than Occidental Park in Pioneer Square, and not as attractive. But, like Occidental, it is a quiet, pleasant place for those sleeping something off by day, and it is difficult and potentially dangerous by night. A flash point, thus, as the developers of Marvin Gardens must have known, and they went ahead and built there anyway. Designed by the Driscoll Architects, it is a five-story building of red, green, and blue, all muted so it doesn't seem new and blends in swell with its surroundings. Was it lunatic to build there? courageous? prescient? Since Marvin Gardens is one of the very few good looking new apartment/condo buildings in the Regrade, I hope it keeps its tenants and finds new mates, because the one thing that will make or keep the problem in the park manageable is a critical mass of residents, people on the streets at night.

On Fourth your main task is to find places from which you can get good views of Martin Selig's black, shiny buildings, the Fourth and Blanchard, Fourth and Battery, and Fourth and Vine, the architect of record being Chester Lindsey. My responses are a motley: since all the blending and harmonizing in the area are done at ground level and the other tall buildings just stick up in the air, these do better here than they would elsewhere; the statement they make, "These are my buildings, not yours," is made with such confidence that in fact they helped Selig get tenants and forced surrounding owners to think they could do more with their property than let it sit there; the black, the odd shapes on the Fourth and Battery, the arrogant sheets of glass, have a kind of deep city unfriendliness that is not altogether unattractive; you get a nice reflection of the Space Needle on the Fourth and Vine Building.

As you muse on the Selig phenomena, you probably walk right by the Two Bells Tavern, between Bell and Battery; it has the perfect understated Regrade exterior, lunch and dinner inside, cheap, lots of beers. Then on almost any street between Battery and Vine turn left and go back to Second and turn left again. By the time you reach Bell, the 211 Club on your left now, you are in the mini-area its denizens call Belltown, an arts community of sorts that needs to depend on inexpensive rents to see what it can become. The buildings here are nondescript, and probably date from 1910–20, though there was a Belltown here in the last century. On the west side of the street past Bell, the Wall of Sound; on the east, past Mama's Mexican Kitchen and the Thai House Restaurant, are Hula's Collectibles and the Dingo Gallery, full of this and that and also home of the AHA! Theatre. Next to the Dingo's is the Signature Bound Bookseller, which opens at noon and stays open late, the prevailing habit of Belltown. The Two Bells Tavern ought to be somewhere here on Second instead of over on Fourth. Things change so rapidly here—the Rive Gauche restaurant and Seattle Fine Books departed in 1993, and the AFL-CIO sponsored Concept One Apartments have gone up— that that too may happen. Finally, on the corner, is the clean, well-lighted Crocodile Cafe, live music at night.

The Regrade, it should be clear, can tolerate a great deal of mix and match, as on First and Second especially, or mix and not

Two Bells Tavern, perfect understated Regrade exterior,
lunch and dinner inside, lots of beers

match, as with the Darth Vader buildings. These last are brimming with vitality compared to the one thing the Regrade should not be asked to tolerate, namely the almost windowless U.S. West Building on the northwest corner of Second and Lenora. It should have been built a hundred feet underwater in Elliott Bay, on First Hill among the hospitals, or in some Eastside "park" surrounded by trees. Not here, across from the Belltown Center, across from the worn but still lovely terra cotta of Bethel Temple (designed as a natatorium by B. Marcus Priteca), whose readerboard admonishes us unthreateningly.

New life that does not threaten old life, new life that awakens and enhances old life. You don't even have to be particularly careful about building here, as you must be in Pioneer Square or along First further south. There's plenty of land; you could build a small city of low-rise apartments on the existing car lots between Stewart and Denny, First and Fifth. Change here has been gradual, and mostly unplanned; the public sector has needed to do no more than some rezoning to allow for more residences, issue permits, and maintain services. Of these, nighttime safety in Regrade Park has perhaps been the most difficult. Change also continues. As long as development continues on the scale and the pace it has had, the next twenty years could be great for the Regrade.

SEATTLE COMMONS

There is no clear eastern boundary to the Denny Regrade, but starting at some point east of Fifth and the Monorail tracks, and extending down to Westlake and up the slope to Fairview, running north-south from Lake Union to the edge of downtown is a large parcel of underused land, much of which now lies vacant and most of the rest of which is warehouse space for wholesalers.

Arriving just as the most recent boom was ending in Seattle came trumpets and hautboys announcing dreams, then plans, for a very ambitious project that has as its goal the transformation of this land into a large public park, on the model of Central Park in New York, to be surrounded by the Seattle equivalents of the Dakota Apartments, the Plaza Hotel, if not the Metropolitan Museum. Some of those playing the music are well-known former public officials whose past achievements are worthy and whose good intentions are unquestionable. Stand at some convenient spot, looking north on Westlake from near the Westin Hotel, or on the bluff near the Seattle Times buildings on Fairview, and imagine all this could be. As of this writing, the hope is to have this project completed by the turn of the century, and, the implication has been, only carpers, naysayers, and property owners with other aims will object.

Almost at the other end of the present century, a famous civil engineer and planner, Virgil Bogue, was hired by the City of Seattle to make some plans. Inside the two large volumes Bogue presented were descriptions of much that came to pass, like Aurora Avenue and the heart of the Port of Seattle at the mouth of the Duwamish River, and much more that did not, like the creation of a huge public park on Mercer Island. The centerpiece of the Bogue plan was a government complex, designed to look something like the Piazza San Marco in Venice, to be placed near where Seattle Center was eventually situated. Bogue's plans were put to a vote, and defeated, most of the money for the opposition coming from property owners in lower downtown, near where the government buildings then were and still are. A vision created, a vision shunned, just when Seattle's first boom was ending. The players of the trumpets and hautboys have this tune in their repertoire.

To the user of a guidebook, none of this need matter if plans for Seattle Commons, as the project is called, do not come to fruition, and, if they do, then an entry different from this one will be needed. If only as a means of encouraging, in this matter as in many others in this book, a dynamic relation between enthusiasm and criticism, I offer three interlocking caveats about the plans. First, the timing is terrible. Such a project to be successful probably needs to be completed in almost all its phases, which means great expenditures of public funds. In periods of economic quiescence, one gets around putting the matter to a vote by cutting deals as well as corners, building on spec as well as on the cheap, encouraging the wrong development by the wrong developers. Second, New York's Central Park, like other large eastern city parks, was a perfect expression for the class that owned carriages and cars a century ago. Currently many such parks are sufficiently dangerous at night as to force wealthy neighbors into building fortresses, and thereby to create gaps and suspicions where amelioration and toleration are essential. Third, many times more often than not American cities have come to grief when they have allowed planning on this large a scale, if only because grand and visionary planning easily loses sight of the day-to-day consequences of what might look good on a drawing board. Look back on the great achievements and legacies of either of Seattle's two great boom periods and you'll see, over and over, places where money, energy, and land of a size commensurate for the money and energy met. None of these conditions currently hold for the creation of a Seattle Commons anything like, or anything as good as, its planners plan or its dreamers dream.

I place this note at the end of this chapter not just because the Seattle Commons land is adjacent to that of Denny Regrade but also because the Regrade is the best current example of good things happening *because* they're happening in fits and starts, bit by bit, as suits the land in question as well as the money and energy currently available.

6 Seattle Center and Lower Queen Anne

Though this is one of the most frequently visited sections of Seattle, by Seattle people as well as visitors, it may be among the least looked at. Seattle Center was created for Century 21, the 1962 World's Fair, and though most of what was built was intended to outlast the fair, some was done on the cheap, and at a time when there was no major league sport in Seattle, and interest in the performing arts was much less than it is now. So there have been plans and proposals, but none of them started from the proposition that the place is something of a miracle among ex–world's fair grounds, and is a resounding success. Perhaps this is because its daytime and nighttime visitors are so different from each other, or perhaps because people may be anticipating or wanting some isolated facility surrounded by parking for 10,000 cars (Dodger Stadium in Chavez Ravine, or Disneyland in Anaheim) and do not see that there really are lots of nearby parking lots or that lower Queen Anne north and west of the Center is one of the most viable "urban villages" in the city.

Seattle's signature structure

This is a classic case of that which is not broken not needing to be fixed.

The walk is best done when you have a whole afternoon, and can spend lots of time at the Science Center, or a whole evening, and can see some game or performance and walk before and after.

Walk: one hour, not including time spent indoors.
Bus: monorail from Westlake Center, or #1 or #2 bus from Third Avenue to First Avenue North and Thomas.

If you take the monorail, you will emerge looking straight up at the Space Needle; if you take the bus, it will come into view as you walk east on Thomas toward it.

The Space Needle is Seattle's signature structure, and we could have done far worse. It was designed for the fair in 1962 by the John Graham Company (initial conceptual design sketches by Victor Steinbrueck), and back then I sensed that while people loved to go up and catch the great views they were a trifle embarrassed about the way it looked. For myself the sentiment has been reversed. I seldom go up—and whatever you do, go to the observation deck and not the restaurant—but love to find new places from which to have a look at the Needle, though my favorites remain Volunteer Park and Williams Place (the postage stamp park across 15th Avenue East from Group Health) on Capitol Hill. Two reasons help account for this shift in feeling: one, its vertical lines have come to seem more graceful than the skyscrapers downtown that stress verticality; two, after the creation of Star Trek's *Enterprise,* the Space Needle's space ship came to seem pleasantly of its post-Sputnik time when most space ships and all UFOs looked like this one.

If you're at the base of the Needle, you'll see two sculptures,

Alexander Liberman's *Olympic Iliad* and Lauren Ewing's *Endless Gate,* both work of the mid-1980s. Both to my mind are "interesting" more than successful, but the Center is filled with sculptures and you need not agree with my sense that they are always better if they include water.

At the south end of the Center is the Pacific Science Center, identifiable by its white arches. Even if you are doing this walk in the evening, after the place is closed, it is well worth a look. It is the work of Minoru Yamasaki, also responsible for the IBM Building and the Security Pacific Tower downtown; I find this much more successful than either of those. Yamasaki's task was to build five windowless buildings to house exhibits and theaters, and he has done it so well you have to think twice to see what his original challenge was. In the middle, arches, pools, steps; the buildings at the edges, unobtrusive. None of which has anything to do with science, but that hardly matters. Could it be that it expresses many westerners' idea of "Japanese" without its actually being that? Whatever. People respond to it as they should, by keeping their voices down, so that except when there are ten buses outside loaded with school kids, the loudest sound is the water.

Inside (hours 10–6 daily, admission charge) is room after room of hands-on activities, mazes and puzzles, tests and displays; only in the IMAX Theater is one allowed to go completely passive. It is a long way from "science" as any kind of organized activity, but it is a sour person on a sour day who will not find one or two things simply captivating.

Outside of the Science Center, daytime activities at Seattle Center are mostly the carnival rides near the Space Needle and whatever is happening at the Center House (formerly called the Food Circus), which is directly in front of you as you leave the Science Center. One glance at either will tell you if it is of inter-

Yamasaki's arches at the Pacific Science Center

est to you. Nighttime, everything is on the north and west edges: working from left to right, the Coliseum (NBA basketball primarily), the Bagley Wright Theatre (Seattle Repertory), the Playhouse (Intiman Theatre), the Opera House (Seattle Symphony, Seattle Opera, Pacific Northwest Ballet), the Arena (Western Hockey League); Memorial Stadium (high school football and soccer).

Day or night, have a look at the Science Center and then move north, past the Center House and the fountain, toward the arenas. Especially in the early evening there is a fine feeling of people gathering, gathering to watch very different things, dressed differently, walking at different paces. The buildings from the outside are mostly just passable, except for the Bagley Wright Theatre, typical brutal work by NBBJ and totally heedless of its sur-roundings, and for Paul Thiry's Coliseum, the best sports arena in the area.

When water is used, it is good. In addition to Yamasaki's pools and the central fountain, there are Everett DuPen's *Fountain of Creation* between the Coliseum and the conference rooms at the northwest edge of the Center, François Stahly's Julius Lang Memo-rial Fountain in the mall between the Playhouse and Opera House, and especially James FitzGerald's *Fountain of the North-west,* all built for the World's Fair. In addition, in the lobbies of both the Playhouse and the Opera House are lots of paintings, some fine, but these can be seen only if you are going to a perfor-mance; if you are, see the huge Mark Tobey, *Journey of the Opera Star,* a fascinating rather than moving work, but amply interesting for a full intermission's scrutiny. It is in the entrance foyer of the Opera House. Guy Anderson's *Cultural Fragments* in the first-balcony foyer is good too.

Daytime or nighttime, emerge from between the Opera House and Playhouse and turn left (west) on Mercer. It may not matter much how you proceed. I suggest turning left on First North, right on Republican, right on Queen Anne Avenue, left on Mercer to First West, right to Roy, right on Roy, where you can make your way back to the bus on Queen Anne Avenue or through the Center to the monorail. There is nothing here you must see. The basic residential building here is the two- to four-story apartment (there are some larger ones on the south slope of the hill), which gives the neighborhood an unusually high population density for Seattle. Since public transportation is good here, many of these people do not own a car. In the QFC just north of the Center is a parking lot that a respectable suburban supermarket would be ashamed to call one, since it holds only a couple of dozen cars. But lower Queen Anne is a village, not some planner's sentimental dream of one, so the QFC is full of people who walk to and from market. A friend who works in the bakery there says her clientele is more varied than she finds in QFCs on Capitol Hill or near the University.

By day the pace is neighborhoody, neither sleepy nor crowded, but active and unobtrusive. By night the action emanates from the Center, from the Uptown Cinemas on Queen Anne and A Contemporary Theatre (ACT) on Roy, to pizza, to the fast lane bar at Duke's down on First Avenue West, to Tower Books and Tower Records, which stay open until midnight. It is as busy as any nighttime neighborhood in the city, and because busy, safe, the sine qua non of good places after dark. It is not a neighborhood to get rhapsodic about, because it is plain and unimpressed with itself, but the moment you stop taking it for granted you can find it gets ever more interesting and appealing.

Queen Anne Avenue in a premier urban village

97   SEATTLE CENTER AND LOWER QUEEN ANNE

7 Chinatown International District

The double designation expresses a tension, though not primarily the one you might think, between the Chinese and Chinese Americans and all the other Asian ethnic groups who live or work in the neighborhood. There is another, between those who got the area established as a Historic District, who want the buildings to stay the same, and white money and businesses kept out as much as possible (they tend to like the more politically correct "International District"), and those who regret seeing people move away as soon as they can afford to, who stress that the living conditions are often inadequate, who would be happy to see investment from the outside (and who know that "Chinatown" is a good enough name for similar areas in many American cities, so why not here?). Thus the slash, and the public corporation Chinatown/International District Development Authority, which governs much of what does and does not happen in the area.

For a long time alongside Chinatown was Japantown, which centered on Jackson, and ran up the hill to Main and then Yesler. The pre–World War II Yesler Terrace housing project, the railroading off of Japanese Americans to camps during the war, the

I-5 freeway, and the tendency of many Japanese Nisei to assimilate in other parts of the county, destroyed Japantown. In the last decade refugees from Southeast Asia have poured into the area; some live and work in the Historic District; others have jumped the freeway barrier and established Little Saigon, centered on 12th and Jackson; still others have set up Littler Saigon near Franklin High School in Rainier Valley. Chinese from China, Hong Kong, Taiwan, and Singapore continue to come into the area, and the Chinese are clearly the dominant presence.

Chinatown/ID is isolated by the strength of its boundaries—Yesler on top of the hill to the north, the I-5 freeway to the east, Dearborn and I-90 to the south, Fifth Avenue and the railroad tracks to the west. It is also isolated by its traditions and languages, and by its dependence on them. The result, in truth, is a small city of its own, economically dependent on people from surrounding Seattle to buy its food, uncooked and cooked, in restaurants and groceries, but otherwise it must provide for itself, at least at the level of goods and services.

You can walk every foot of the International District in a little more than an hour. What you will be looking at is retail businesses at ground level, two to four stories of apartments above, almost the entire time. I want to vary the usual way of these walks. First, I list some of the goods and services one would expect or hope to find in a small city and ask you to find them here if you can; I do not promise to produce them all. Then I name places that are worth more than casual attention. Make your own route. The east-west streets run Main, Jackson, King, Weller, Lane. The north-south streets are Fifth, Sixth, Maynard, Seventh, Eighth. By bus, take anything coming south in the bus tunnel to the International District. As you emerge, Chinatown faces you across Fifth and you can move up South Jackson. Driving, you'll find spaces without meters going up the hill on

Sixth and Seventh, and on top on Main. It can be hard to find any kind of parking on weekends, when families from throughout the area come for lunch and shopping at Uwajimaya; it is also liveliest then.

As you walk, see if you can find a pharmacy, a law office, a travel agent, an architect, a pet store, a movie theater, a furniture store, a computer store, automobile repair, a gas station, a church, a copier, a post office, a liquor store, an insurance agent, a hardware store, a place to buy needle and thread, a photo finisher, a photographer. Looking for these, you are bound to become alert to the activities of this city.

The following are listed alphabetically.

Alps Hotel, 615–625 South King. This six-story building is about as large as any in the neighborhood, but in other ways it conforms to the type. It was always known as a workingman's hotel—or as a way station for railroad passengers—and so it still is, in its upper stories. It was designed in 1910 by the estimable John Graham, and you will see many instances of similar hotels of the same period built without Graham's ability to supply classy touches to the exterior.

Chong Wa Benevolent Association, 522 Seventh South. The architect of this 1929 building is unknown, but it is one of few in the area that was Asian from its first breath, and used by the same organization for the same purposes since its inception. By 1929, the area had become Chinatown, and that could happen. In those days the family and benevolent organizations were crucial to the ongoing life of the neighborhood, and this is one of the few such organizations that still has much day-to-day influence.

Governor Apartments, 514–526 South Jackson. This is the home of the Mikado Restaurant on its southwest end, but also the nice work of J. L. McCauley, who designed a number of attractive hotels in the area in the 1920s. Since you will see mostly functional design in this neighborhood, do note the terra-cotta decorations here, and the fine balustrade on top.

Hing Hay Park, corner of South King and Maynard South. This has become the focal point of Chinatown since it was designed and created in 1973, principally by Donald Sakuma. This also was Asian from its first breath, and has nothing like the reputation for nighttime danger or unpleasantness of Occidental or Regrade parks. Some South King Street restaurants are open late, so it may help that people are on the streets right there. Early in the morning you might find a little vegetable marketing here, and during the day it tends to elderly men quietly talking and smoking.

International District Children's Park, Seventh South and South Lane. This park, designed by Joey Ing in 1982, is highlighted by a dragon play structure by sculptor Gerard Tsutakawa. If you want to see how kids use it, the best time is afternoons after school on dry days; on weekends and during summer it is quiet.

International District Community Garden, hillside north of South Main. The ultimate urban P-patch. The garden is 1.5 acres, the gardeners are all elderly, low-income Chinatown/ID residents, and there are now 120 gardens. Go in late fall and winter to see how much is growing; go in summer to see how much more, including runner beans and other vines. Amazingly productive. Kobe Terrace Park, with nice views, is alongside.

International House, southeast corner Maynard South and South Weller. This was designed in the 1980s by Chester Lindsey, Martin Selig's architect. A perfectly ordinary low-rise apartment building, it is of consequence here because it is the only new building inside the Historic District's boundaries, and therefore represents an effort to bring or keep middle-income residents in

an area where the residents are mostly poor. It's especially instructive because it stands across Maynard from the New Century Hotel, where twenty-eight units of low-income residences were created in a 1984 restoration by Burke Associates working with federal Block Grant funds. Phase II, rehabilitation at the street level, was planned but never enacted. One possible conclusion: reliance on public money can be a dubious proposition; a companion is that it will be hard to get private money to renovate in Chinatown/ID unless new construction is allowed. Part of the tension mentioned at the outset is surely at work here.

Little Saigon, underneath I-5, up South Jackson, mostly between 11th and 14th. It is doubtful that any earlier wave of immigrants from anywhere made such a sudden visual impact on Seattle as Southeast Asians have here. As is the case down the hill, the main thing going is food, but the proliferation, the amazing reuse of small spaces, is phenomenal. A dozen years ago this area comprised primarily a liquor store and Connor's, an appliance store that had been gritting its teeth as its customers left the area. Then came Jackson Square, a dozen shops and eateries, and Little Asia, a dozen more. I doubt even if all Chinatown residents know how to make their way up here, but this has the kind of vitality that can astonish. Have a look, have a meal.

Tsue Chong Noodle Factory, 801–811 South King. They make nineteen different Chinese noodles here, and they would be happy to sell you any kind, but somewhat less happy to be asked to play tour guide of all nineteen. I suggest you look and point.

Uwajimaya, Sixth South and South King. You can start by calling this a supermarket, which it is, and a good one, whose local customers include residents of Pioneer Square as well as the

Hing Hay Park

Uwajimaya, where you can have a wonderful time without spending a dime

International District. You can add that Uwajimaya knows that the equivalent of the Pike Place Market lies in Chinatown's small groceries, and it wants to compete with these, also with the estimable Mutual Fish Company out on Rainier Avenue South, also with any Asian or black butcher when it comes to various animal parts and organs, and to assure the large chains that for Asian bottled and canned goods they just don't get it. There is also a sushi and deli takeout. You can have a wonderful time here without spending a dime.

Wing Luke Asian Museum, 407 Seventh South. Wing Luke was Seattle's first Asian American elected official, and might have become its first Asian American mayor had he not been killed in an airplane crash in 1965. The aim of this museum, which charges a modest fee, is to offer exhibits that explain aspects of Asian art, life, and history—to other Asians, and to the rest of us. You should be able to tell from the displays outside if a particular exhibit is appealing to you.

About the restaurants. I have been told by people who eat here regularly that you need never eat a bad meal in Chinatown, and the secret is not so much where to go as what to order. If you throw yourself on the good offices of your waiter you may be given standard tourist fare, but you will probably be treated better than if you try to manage the large menu, especially since often what is best is not on the menu. Holes-in-the-wall can be good, and so too places that seat 600. The best way to be treated well is to go to one place regularly, and to always order soup in Thai and other Southeast Asian restaurants.

8 Queen Anne Hill

Here we are out of downtown entirely, looking down on all we have thus far seen. Before the turn of the century a streetcar line ran out First Avenue, past the land claims of pioneers David Denny and Thomas Mercer, to the foot of Queen Anne Hill, the city's tallest and steepest. After the hill was logged off, a few mansions were built on the southern slope. In those days when people built for a view, more often than not it was downtown they wanted to see, not water and mountains. First Hill, just east of downtown, was developed similarly at that time, but it was an exclusive neighborhood, as Queen Anne never has been. As a result, when the newer rich made their homes farther out, above Lake Washington and in The Highlands, First Hill faded and Queen Anne never did. Even on what people think of as the "best" Queen Anne streets, Eighth West and West Highland, there are houses of different ages and degrees of grandness, and every-where south of the north slope the houses are pleasant and ordinary for the most part.

There are places of note outside the scope of the two walks I'm proposing. Queen Anne Avenue itself has become one of Seattle's best neighborhood commercial streets. Just north of the corner

Looking east from Queen Anne hill: Gas Works Park on the shore of Lake Union, houseboats on the far side, Lake Washington and the Cascades in the distance of Fifth North and Lynn is one of Seattle's least known great views, looking north and east. Perhaps it is most remarkable for showing different bodies of fresh water, from the Ship Canal through Lake Union, Portage Bay, the Montlake Cut, Union Bay, and Lake Washington, spread out the way they are on a map. On the back wall of the Queen Anne branch of the public library, 400 West Garfield, is *Quintet in D,* an amusing stained glass painting by Richard Spaulding.

Walk 1: forty minutes.
Bus: #2 from Third and Pike to Fourth West and West Galer.

This walk concentrates on the southwest slope of Queen Anne. It does not take long, and if you are full of energy it can easily be incorporated into the longer Walk 2 below. As you get off the bus or out of your car and walk west on Galer, the major object in view is West Queen Anne Elementary School, built in 1896, closed for more than two decades. It looks as if it could still be a school, or a community or senior center like other closed schools in Seattle. It is actually apartments—good, not luxurious—designed by Val Thomas, who lives on the top floor, and stands as a model of a recycled old building in a residential neighborhood.

Turn left on Sixth, and go down a block to West Lee. On your left are two beautifully spreading European chestnut trees; on your right, the street trees are elms. Walking up the hill on Lee we come to the only house and grounds in Seattle to occupy an entire city block. As a house, inside or out, it is like those on Millionaire Row on Capitol Hill—a dark, gloomy mansion. Standing at the foot of the drive, you can feel you are sneaking up on something, but even if the gate were not locked, how far could you get up the drive before guard dogs barked? What I take to be a Colorado spruce stands up 75 feet in the middle of a parking circle. I know there must be great views from the sides of the house I cannot see, but the same views are available further on. You can embrace any feeling you have of being shut out, and say out loud that the trees, like the moon, belong to everyone.

Up Lee, turn right on Willard, back to Galer, turn left. At Seventh, Galer becomes three tiers of stairs downhill. At the top of the stairs on your left are three weeping Sierra redwoods, very striking, while on your right is a regular one of the species. Near the bottom of the steps, on your left is a noble beech, a tree you can look up into from various steps and find as interesting as most human faces. Then you are out on Eighth.

The long concrete wall on the other side of Eighth was designed by W. R. B. Willcox in 1913. It is your clue that the property on the east side is so much in possession of the ultimate building sites that its owners isolated themselves from folk lower on the slope with this fine, slightly ornate wall. Surprisingly, then, you'll find the houses are quite unannouncing affairs. Right at the foot of the steps, 1432 is the most ambitious, and its rectangles manage to make it look too much like a fortress. There is a fine copper beech nearby, but mostly you want to be looking south and west, ending up at a small viewpoint.

Officially this is Marshall Park, but the only named designation is Betty Bowen Viewpoint. Victor Steinbrueck designed this to honor Bowen, who lived down the hill from here, and who had supported artists and the Art Museum in many ways, culminating, perhaps, in her book, *Tobey's 80,* in 1970. He asked nine artists to submit paintings and sketches, then he and the Olympia Stone Company had them and his own cast into concrete panels to form a semicircle at the Viewpoint. Since the artists include all the Northwest's heavy hitters—Tobey, Graves, Anderson, Callahan—it makes for quite an array, subdued, impres-

The emperor view from Kerry Park

sive. There is also a James Washington sculpture of two birds, and, down below, a sitting area designed by Leo Kenney, with his panel in the center. And the view itself is one of the best of central Puget Sound, worth your making sure to take this walk on a sunny day when the Olympics are out.

Kitty-corner from the viewpoint is lovely Parsons' Gardens, a 1956 gift to the city by children of their parents' family garden. It is elegantly kept up, and if you would like to get married here, call the City Parks and Recreation Department.

You are now on West Highland Drive, known as one of the great residential streets of Seattle. Do not ask too much of it, because it has no great houses and its having been built and rebuilt in every decade of the century means nothing harmonizes very well. Still, it's a fun place to be, and a few blocks down the street, on the right, is Kerry Park, a wonderful viewpoint that complements the Betty Bowen. Smack dab in the middle of the view here is the Space Needle, equidistant from Two Union Square and the Washington Mutual Tower; this is a good place to see how graceful the Needle can look. Having said you should see Betty Bowen on a sunny day, I add you should see this view after dark. You are much closer to downtown here than you are seeing it from Gas Works Park or Duwamish Head, and you are also above the scene, looking down. I call it the Emperor View, and no emperor ever saw better.

When I began teaching in Seattle, I asked my students where they had gone to high school, to get a sense of where they were from and how that might have contributed to their being who they were. I became aware that students from Queen Anne High often had a sense of themselves as city people, and this in an era when much of Seattle wanted to be suburban. On this walk, and especially from Kerry Park, I can sense why. This is another residential area—good houses, nothing commercial nearby, but it has a city feel, because it is linked to the expanse of "downtown," from the Center to the Dome. This may be why West Highland Drive has gained a reputation that, taken house by house, it might not seem to deserve.

The best road to take you back to Galer is Fourth West.

Walk 2: forty-five minutes, or two hours.
Bus: #13 from Third and Pike to Third West and West McGraw.

On most good maps of Seattle, a group of streets on the top of Queen Anne are usually marked as if outlining a route. This is known as Queen Anne Boulevard. Some of it was laid out by the Olmsteds (for Olmsteds see Chapters 11–13), and since West Highland is one of the Boulevard's southern borders, you could start right there, and follow it around. I suggest, however, that you start on its north border, and move clockwise. The point of this walk is the grand and almost unbroken array of street trees. You could come here to meditate deeply, or play urban horticulturist; but equally easily you could come for conversation with one or two others, and register the trees primarily as atmosphere. What I can offer here is just an itinerary, and say what streets have what trees.

Start, then, at Five Corners Hardware Store, on the corner of Third West, West McGraw, and West McGraw Place, and take the latter street. For the most part the Boulevard tells you its route; the first streets to follow after McGraw Place are Fifth West, West Raye (alongside Mount Pleasant Cemetery, which has gravestones dating from the last century), Eighth West, West Fulton, 10th West, West Wheeler, and Eighth for a block back to West McGraw. If you want to identify trees along the way, notable is a yellow birch on Eighth near the cemetery. A little further on, near Eighth and West Fulton, is a large black cherry, and West Fulton is lined with European white elms east of Ninth. Along 10th West, before you get to West Halladay are many pin oaks. Further along on 10th and on West Wheeler are many bigleaf lindens, and a couple of yellow buckeyes (horse chestnuts) can be found on Wheeler east of Ninth, and on McGraw east of Eighth.

This much will take you about forty-five minutes. If that is enough, you can walk east on McGraw back to Third. To continue on, turn right at Seventh, then drop down to Eighth at Blaine, go along the concrete wall its entire length to West Highland, continue on Highland across Queen Anne Avenue and climb up until Bigelow North begins and angles off to the left. Bigelow is one of the two or three best streets in the city for trees, most notably a variety of oaks at its outset here, and then a great many European chestnuts as it curves northward. The route continues via Wheeler, Third North, McGraw, McGraw Place, Smith, McGraw Place again, and at the triangle formed by First West, West Smith, and West McGraw Place are two handsome downy hawthorns. You may have noted that all the trees listed here are deciduous, but do not on that account think this is not a good walk in winter. Leafless of course gives a different feel to these streets, but the lindens are at their best that way, and of the others only the chestnuts are inferior.

9 Capitol Hill

When Seattle began, it was part of the Oregon Territory, and one of pioneer Arthur Denny's first dreams was that Seattle would become the capitol when Washington became its own territory. To that end he made a plat of one of the hills east of his original land claim and called it Capitol Hill. All quite fanciful, since Seattle was barely ten years old when Washington did become a territory and Seattle was given the university, which eventually was to be much more important than a capitol.

As for Capitol Hill, it was virgin timber when Denny named it, but Henry Yesler worked relentlessly at logging the land east of the city. Yesler Way was the original Skid Road down which logs were slid. By the time it had a streetcar line built up it, much of the land on First and Capitol hills had been logged and people were building houses there, some very grand. Then a street-car was built out Broadway from Yesler to City Park (after the Spanish-American War, renamed Volunteer Park), near the north slope of Capitol Hill. Mansions were built to the west of the park, on the slope above Lake Union, in what is now the Harvard-Belmont Historic District. Commerce built up along the streetcar line. In the early years of this century James A. Moore (who put his own name on theaters on Second Avenue and East Pine) developed many streets east of 15th, and soon there followed those pillars of the Catholic Church, St. Joseph Church and Holy Names Academy. In 1916, Nellie Cornish opened the Cornish School of the Arts across from Broadway High School; in 1921 it moved to its present location, a handsome stucco building on East Roy. Fred Anhalt developed a number of superb brick apartments on Capitol Hill in the 1920s, which was also when St. Mark's Episcopal Cathedral on 10th was begun. Between then and the citywide changes of the 1970s and 1980s, the one major change was Group Health Cooperative establishing itself in the old St. Luke's Hospital on 15th East, from whence it has become the largest member-run, locally operated health maintenance organization in the country. Visually not a great deal has changed on Capitol Hill in the last generation, but the feel of much of it is different because the feel of Broadway is different.

Twenty-five years ago Broadway was like North 45th in Wallingford, or Queen Anne Avenue, a solid commercial street, mostly serving the neighborhood but blessed with two good furniture and household item stores in Keeg's and Del Teet's, which could bring people in from anywhere. Starting in the 1970s, but continuing at an accelerating rate through the 1980s, it became a street like no other in the city, much the liveliest place to be at night, the center for a much more visible gay community (for information of gay meeting and gathering, call *Gay News*) and home to more places where you can spend money per square foot than any street this side of San Francisco. I recently counted 128 on the six blocks between Denny and Roy, and that does not include places on the immediate side streets. This is not a street where I can in good conscience propose a walk wherein I will show you what you might enjoy looking at. In one sense, don't look, because solemnly stared at an awful lot of Broadway turns out to be either junk or dead level ordinary—fast food joints, pizza, photocopiers, video stores, convenience stores. At a time when most neighborhoods in the older parts of Seattle are gaining fairly ambitious good-value restaurants, Broadway spits these out as if they were a bad taste. (But where else could you find both a Mongolian and a Tibetan restaurant? And in the main six blocks there are five Thai restaurants.) There is a fair amount of panhandling. Almost nothing is pleasing in the look of the buildings or the store windows.

Still, you must go, not to meditate and conclude or decide, but to be there, to see and be seen if that is your scene. Things are stirring on Broadway around 7 a.m., and by midmorning the sidewalks are crowded, the traffic slow. It is still going at midnight, which means that while you might well meet some unsavory looking people here, no one ever need feel in danger. The street, like the neighborhood, is predominantly white, but there is a good mix of others too. Here there is Dilettante Chocolates, where the product is sold on a principle usually found only in New York—namely, charge twice fair market value and people will happily pay. Then up a block is Pilgrim Congregational, which finds many ways to help the homeless. Franchises hang on to Broadway like leeches, but most shops are one of a kind, and this is assuredly as good a place as any to try to operate on a shoestring. On Broadway any junky cafe will be jammed with the young, especially if they can order just coffee or sit outdoors. Street corners are places of meeting and talking. People embrace, people quarrel. You can see any kind of dress, including drag and the business suit, and some kinds of undress. So, after a good dinner in some other part of town, walk it off on Broadway.

There is a good echo of Broadway on the commercial stretch of 15th East, also between Denny and Roy, and a fainter echo still on 19th East, centered on the corner of East Aloha, where the scene is dominated by St. Joseph Church.

On the north slope of Capitol Hill are Interlaken and Boren parks, sixty acres of beautiful second-growth forest. Within two hundred yards of getting off a #12 bus at 19th and East Galer and going down Interlaken Drive or any of the unpaved paths, you can feel you have left the city entirely. The main road is Interlaken Boulevard, excellent for biking and jogging as well as walking. In winter you have views to the north, but it is best when leaves are on the trees and you can feel surrounded by green. All this was created first by George Cotterill, who planned a series of bicycle trails—this one to extend from Volunteer Park to Washington Park. Almost two decades later, when they got around to giving this forest a name, they saw that Carson Boren's daughter Louisa was the only original white settler alive, so they named it after her. Years later still, Victor Steinbrueck designed a small park at a viewpoint above Louisa Boren Park, at the junction of 15th East, East Garfield, and East Olin Place, and they named *that* after her too. It is a stunning view, complementary to one on the University of Washington campus, also of Union Bay and Lake Washington, but this faces north toward Mount Baker, and that one south toward Mount Rainier.

Perhaps the next day after you have done your stint on Broadway, you can take a long walk on residential Capitol Hill. Along with the two Lake Washington ridge walks, this is the one I would most recommend your doing with those out-of-town visitors who ask what makes Seattle distinctly itself.

Walk: three hours.
Bus: #12 from Pike Street to 19th East and East Galer.

The question to be asked here, right after "What do you make of this house?" is "What is the relation of this house to its neigh-bors?" From 19th East and East Galer go east a block and a half on Galer. It is a fine street, but it's in looking at 2010 that I want to ask our questions. It is Mediterranean style stucco, looking more Italian than Spanish with its sculptured cypress trees. It is a style that may seem "out of place" in a land of gray skies and conifers, but this one is stunningly successful, wonderfully designed windows especially, a mansion so confident that it seems to make its much more modest neighbors irrelevant. It's as though 2010 can fill up the entire picture. Just the opposite circumstance obtains up the street, at 2103 and 2109. Here you have two houses that were not designed as a pair but have become one over the years, perhaps by cooperative acts, perhaps by a later house painter deciding to harmonize with an earlier one. You get a blend, not a match, and the good fence here almost certainly makes good neighbors. Go back west on Galer, cross the arterial on 19th, and you'll notice Stevens Elementary School, the 1906 design of James Stephen, which has hand-somely survived a major onslaught from Catholic families' sending their children to St. Joe's up the street half a century ago, and the general decline in Seattle's schools in more recent times. As a building it is nice—wood frame, massive classic entrance—but lots of schools of its 1900–1920 era looked as good and now are closed.

As you continue walking west on Galer to 17th and turn left, you might then feel that good houses and good streets yield good schools, a fact rare enough not to be scorned, but hardly exciting visually until you come to the southeast corner of 17th and Highland. First, note a pair of old birches. The trees, it turns out, match two houses, 1158 and 1154, a nesting pair in green wood and stucco, made more remarkable by 1154's being set back fifty feet or so from the street. It must have been a garage

once, and now it looks as if it might be the nicer of the two
to live in. Continue south on 17th. When you get to 1620 East
Prospect, on the corner, you will, I hope, have seen enough large
houses like this one that the term "ordinary mansion" can begin
to make sense. If you then continue down to Aloha, turn right
and walk a block. On the northeast and southwest corners you
have a matched pair of "ordinary mansions." Granted, mansions
aren't supposed to match, but these do, and clearly the architect
thought one would enhance the other. Note that they aren't
identical.

For one building enhancing another, the two blocks north of
Aloha on 16th might well be the supreme example in Seattle.
These are all part of the tract developed by J. A. Moore, and
the contractor must have had a wonderful time mixing and
matching, singing and echoing, no house sticking out. Two trios
here, 933, 939, 943, and 1147, 1151, 1157, are my favorites. Start
with the basic "Capitol Hill box" design: front porch with the
entrance on the right; inside, a living room and dining room on
the left, and straight ahead a hall leading to the kitchen. Four
corner bedrooms upstairs. On 16th is an enchanting set of variations on that theme. Little shifts, in the living-room bow window,
in the roofline or eave slant, in the top dormer, in the porch balustrade or the fanlight, give one house a signature even as it
blends with the others. The pavement always stays beneath my
feet here on 16th, but just barely. When you reach Highland, turn
left, cross the arterial at 15th and wander your way through
Volunteer Park.

There has been a park here for more than a century, but the
layout as you see it was the work of the Olmsted Brothers, whose
hands did so much to shape the parks and boulevards in pre–
World War I Seattle. There is much that is fine to see in Volunteer
Park, and from Volunteer Park. But since this is a long walk, pri-

Capitol Hill boxes on 16th Avenue E

121   CAPITOL HILL

marily concerned with houses and residential streets, let me content myself by naming the obvious pleasures: the old Seattle Art Museum, designed by Carl Gould in 1932, in the middle of the park, introduced by fine Chinese sculptured camels; as you face the Museum, to your left is a greenhouse conservatory at the end of the street, with a good collection of tropical plants; to your right, a water tower, whose 108 steps you can climb to get views of Seattle as good as those from the Space Needle, which is, incidentally, behind you, looking about as good from here as it ever gets. Between you and the Needle is Isamu Noguchi's *Black Sun,* a huge granite sculpted doughnut, much loved. (The Art Museum has a fee; everything else is free.) You leave the park by winding down the road that runs west from the conservatory and the statue of William Henry Seward. About a hundred yards past the tennis courts, when a paved path goes up to the left, take the unpaved one to the right, down a set of steps, past a couple of grand European beeches, to East Highland Drive, whose first cross street is Federal Avenue East.

Turn right, walk down to Blaine on one side, then back on the other. Federal is a famous street, and for a long time I used to take visitors here and wonder why I didn't like it more. The houses are in a variety of styles and building materials—all traditional, all expensive. All architect designed, too, and architects have a tendency to want to do something different and apparently outstanding. No mixing and matching for them. The outstanding houses are enormous stucco ones on the west side, 1254 and an unnumbered one north of East Garfield: double lots, circular driveways, 1254 with a grand fence, the other with a small and oddly inviting doorway entrance. That there is nothing lovable about their way of being impressive does not keep them from being impressive, but I'd rather be up on 16th.

Returning to East Highland Drive, turn right, cross 10th to

Broadway, then gape at 814, which is at least a candidate for the premier house on Capitol Hill. It was built by the Washington, D.C., firm of Hornblower & Marshall for Sam Hill, the railroad baron's son, in 1909, and for decades has been the home of Guendolen Plestcheeff and her Institute for the Decorative Arts. It is for Seattle a very early example of reinforced concrete, painted to look like sandstone. That the house is turned away from the street gives it a snooty feeling that seems entirely appropriate, seeing that it wants to face its view rather than us, but doesn't want to hide the fact with fences.

You are now at the edge of the Harvard-Belmont Historic District, the only such district in the city consisting of residences. Walk south on Harvard East and note houses vying to get your vote, like 1147, the Charles Smith house; and its neighbor, 1137, designed by Carl Gould; the much more recent Bullitt house at 1125, designed by Fred Bassetti in 1955 (it is not easy to see), and a grand pair, 937 and 919. These are not ordinary mansions, each wants to be fairest of them all, take your pick. At East Aloha, turn right, and on your right is a minor masterpiece by Ibsen Nelsen, who designed in the mid-1980s townhouses that look like they are from an earlier era entirely, though there are no attached houses like these in older Seattle. It is not easy to design something new to blend in with this neighborhood, but these do.

Turn left on Boylston East and go far enough to note especially the gate houses on the left; to my mind they are at least as attractive as their masters on Harvard. This is also true a little bit further on; go north on Boylston, then left on Prospect, note the two O. D. Fisher houses (Fisher founded flour mills in the early days) on Belmont, then continue down Prospect to Summit, where the gate houses, designed this time by John Graham, manage to be impressive, but without the heavy gloominess of the main houses. Then a little further down Summit is a splendid

814 Highland, bidding to become the fairest of them all

Townhouses by Ibsen Nelsen in the Havard/Belmont Historic District

antidote to mansions and grandeur. The Bower/Bystrom house, 1022 Summit East, is the oldest house in the neighborhood and one of the oldest in the city. It is very much a house, not a mansion, and has been lovingly kept up, so that it seems both a relic and a house for ordinary folks to live in.

The route goes from Summit left on Bellevue—1001 is a splendidly situated house—then right on Belmont to Roy, left on Roy (where the traffic may be a little heavy). Past Boylston begins an enchanting sequence of buildings. On the left, the stucco of "The Cornish School: Dance, Drama, Music," which was designed by Albertson, Wilson & Richardson (also responsible for St. Joseph Church on 18th) and is now a fully accredited college. The front door is open most of the time; go in and have a little look around, because there is a fine feel of something oxymoronic here, plain elegance. Then across Harvard on the same side is the severely colonial D.A.R. Building, and across from it the Women's Century Club, now the Harvard Exit theater, most notable for a warm and attractive lobby. Finally, back on the north side, the Loveless Block, a building of exquisite taste. In the shops, in the courtyard and surrounding apartments, this is the one place architect Arthur Loveless developed himself, so his name could go onto it, and he could spend his last years here.

Right ahead of you is Broadway, but the Broadway tone is in evidence here only if youth is having coffee outdoors at the Bacchus. Otherwise, a tone that was set by these buildings fifty to seventy years ago prevails.

Cross Broadway, finding Roy again as it crosses 10th, and soon on either side of you are excellent examples of the red brick apartments that Fred Anhalt developed—usually using the designs of Edwin Dofson—on Capitol Hill in the 1920s. Anhalt is like Loveless, a tasteful purveyor of traditional style. You can list the details that seem to matter—steeply pitched roofs, turrets

The Bower/Bystrom house, both a relic and a house for ordinary folks to live in

Courtyard in the Loveless Block

with party hat tops, mullioned windows, on the right a courtyard with a good vicar's garden, on the left a plainer entrance area with two cedars. But, truly, what you are aware of is discretion and grace, excellent siting, not the stylistic details. Your route continues up the hill, Roy becoming a footpath over which a nicely curved bridge connects Lowell Elementary with its playfield, and after you get to 13th East, look to the right to see the Maryland apartments. These, like the Anhalts below, are on the city's landmark register, but the comparison is entirely in Anhalt's favor.

Turn left on 13th East, a mishmash of a street, apartments and houses of various ages, but the road bends nicely. Be sure to note 723 and 727, a pair of houses more modest than any I have noted thus far: identical single-story buildings that partly face each other, years and different owners creating the variations. This is a classic example of what two houses, in this case two that originally sold for well under $10,000, can do for each other.

The next corner is East Aloha, and one block up the hill on it gets you to 14th. On either side of you for about a block is Millionaire Row; if you think you'll like what you'll see, go right down 14th to Roy and back; if not, just go left to Prospect. This seems to me a 1900–1910 instance of what money could buy when buying was all it was doing (recent examples can be found on lower Madrona Drive and N.E. Paisley Drive). Late Victorian architecture was always heavy, tending to gloom, so efforts to compensate were needed, which is why semicircular turrets, with their large windows, are often appealing. Only one turret here, no other attempts to compensate, on Millionaire Row; you'll have to like gloom, and the sense of leather armchair comfort that goes with it, to like this. The trees are good trees, but in leaf make the street seem more claustrophobic still.

One block north of Aloha is Prospect, where you face the Volunteer Park water tower and also the last house on the walk, 1409

East Prospect. You saw a number of ordinary mansions with a similar design early on this walk. This is ordinary raised to the extraordinary: pillars, not two but four and going up not one story but two, the central upstairs windows indicating a two-story hall inside, Chinese dragons on the entrance that echo the great beasts outside the Art Museum. It might be hard to live here, but this is a treat to look at.

If you are traveling by bus, you can catch a #10 to downtown on 15th East; if you parked, it is only a few minutes east on Prospect, then north to Galer on 18th or 19th East. These are more ordinary streets than 17th or 16th, but ordinary may be just what you need after the Harvard-Belmont mansions and Millionaire Row.

What I like about mansions, other than their grandeur if they are grand, is their work in building materials other than wood: when there's money to do something impressive in stucco or stone, fine. But what Seattle does best is the gradations down from mansion, half a dozen or more of them down to the standard old-style bungalow, where the building material is wood, the feeling bourgeois and settled. Capitol Hill as we have seen it here has very little of the lower levels on these gradations, but it has marvelous examples in the upper middle ranges moving on up to the very grand. The pride, one might even say the snobbery, of Capitol Hill is that it could be an island and the rest of Seattle could float out to sea and all would be far from lost. If Capitol Hill could bring itself to see that West Seattle can make the same claim, one could grant its claim, and admire it for the variety of ways it has fulfilled it. Capitol Hill knows little of West Seattle, though. Self-doubt, or even self-scrutiny, is not high on this area's list of attributes. Nonetheless, it could do without us sooner than we could without it.

10 Fremont
Wallingford
North Lake Union

The grand view from Fifth North and Lynn on the northeast slope of Queen Anne is a good place to get your bearings about these neighborhoods. Coming round from the north side of the hill is the ship canal, which was dredged to connect all the fresh water to the east with Salmon Bay and Puget Sound to the west; the locks opened in 1917, the Fremont Bridge, at the east end of the canal, in 1916. There was a town of Fremont before then, plus a small community called Ross on the north slope of Queen Anne, and both were mostly houses for the families of workers in the Stimson shingle mill in Ballard. Ross did not survive the canal and the establishment of Seattle Pacific College on its south shore, but commercial Fremont's old and still very usable buildings were mostly built in the decade after the Fremont Bridge. Residential Fremont extends north up the slope to Woodland Park.

Long before the locks and the canal, developers and speculators Daniel Gilman and Thomas Burke laid the track for a line they called the Seattle, Lake Shore and Eastern, which came out from downtown, around the west and north sides of Queen Anne, then stretched along the north shores of Lake Union and

Fremont, a neighborhood that loves its name

Portage Bay, out to the northern shore of Lake Washington and down to the iron works in Kirkland on the east side. Wallingford developed up the slope from the north shore of Lake Union, now splendidly served by Gas Works Park, just about the most striking landmark in the entire view. Burke also developed a good deal of the area in upper Wallingford, just south of Green Lake, streets whose first letter is K. A few Wallingford houses date from before World War I, but mostly it is 1920s and 1930s stuff.

I want to propose a short walk along the north shore of Lake Union, and while I very much want you to walk in Fremont and Wallingford, I must do my bit somewhat differently.

FREMONT

Bus: #26 from Fourth and Union

Residential Fremont is a very patchy affair, quite a bit inferior to its neighbors to the north and east. There are some perfectly OK stretches, but because it was originally developed for mill workers, those dwellings didn't last. When they were replaced, it was mostly by cheaply built duplexes and apartments in the 1950s and 1960s, which usually blight any neighborhood visually. I mention this at all only because Fremont is famous, primarily for its commerce, granted, but also as a neighborhood. The Fremont Public Association, for instance, is the envy of every community service association in Seattle. Here's a list of its separate operations, each with its own phone number: AIDS Project, Evictions and Deposits, Fair Budget Action Campaign, Family Shelter Program, Food and Housing Services, Food Stamp Outreach, Homecare Program, Housing Development Program, Job Information Line, Mortgage Default Counseling, Resource Development, Welfare Rights Counseling, Worker Center. Of course it may be that it is because residential Fremont is patchy that it needs these services, but this is a place that, as we say, has it together.

Furthermore, no other neighborhood announces its name so frequently in such a small area: Fremont Baptist Church is most visible, perhaps, but just on Fremont Avenue there is also the Fremont Avenue Laundromat, the Fremont Classic Pizzeria, the Fremont Dock Company, the Fremont Mini Warehouse, the Fremont Printing Company, Fremont Terra Cotta, Fremont Mall Antiques, Fremont Flowers, Fremont Place Book Company. Together, and proud to be here.

For the visitor, what's to see is all right there within a four or five block area just north of the Fremont Bridge. Together, proud to be here, but you'll soon note that its businesses are mostly not what anyone would call neighborhood goods and services, and quite a few depend on customers coming from throughout the city or even the county, so specialized is their work. As you walk, then, see if you can sort the strictly neighborhood businesses, like the light grocery on the corner of Fremont North and North 35th, from what might be called the near regional ones, like the Still Life in Fremont Coffeehouse on 35th (always doing brisk business), to the regional ones, like Troll Art, Stampola (creative rubber stamps), and the Dusty Strings Dulcimer Company, a folk instrument manufacturer.

No other neighborhood commercial area in the city reaches out so far for its customers, unless it be the much more urban and less obviously residential Pioneer Square. This gives Fremont its tone of funkiness, its folk art sense of confidence, its not having adapted a smidgeon after the Weyerhaeuser Company's Quadrant Corporation moved in and put up their main building on one side of Fremont Avenue and the Burke Building on the other. Seattle's first recycling operation started here; its first micro-brewery, Redhook Ale Brewery, is a couple of blocks west of Fremont Avenue; and the Fremont street fair is more famous than many larger ones. Upscale is strictly downscale here, at least as much as in Belltown. Funny, though, that these folk don't have something as basic as a pharmacy.

You can walk the area leisurely in half an hour, or if you are attracted to successfully enacted urban minimalism, spend a happy afternoon. You will also need to decide if you like Richard Beyer's *Waiting for the Interurban* sculpture next to the Fremont Bridge. It ranks with the Henry Moore in front of the desolate 1004 Fourth Avenue Building as the city's most famous public sculpture, and since Moore is, after all, Moore, and Beyer is only a local, that says a lot for it. People I admire admire it.

Fremont's relation to the water is not active. There has been talk for years about extending the Burke-Gilman Trail, built over the old Seattle, Lake Shore and Eastern railbed, through Fremont and out into Ballard, but little gets done. What you can do, though, is go over the Fremont Bridge, slip down under it past Wilson Marina, and follow a sort of path next to an old rail line. On your left are parking lots and Seattle Pacific University buildings, but on your right you'll find a row of poplars, the canal, boats, a rope for playing Tarzan or Jane. In a little less than a mile you will come to Ewing Mini Park and Metro's Environmental Lab, and the trail stops.

WALLINGFORD

Bus: #16 from Third and Pike, #26 from Fourth and Union

The dividing line between the two neighborhoods is Stone Way North, a fine nondescript street where people can sell you custom made paint, get it for you wholesale, fix your roof, or get you a deal on a computer or a stereo component.

Residential Fremont, as noted above, and much of what is now industrial Ballard to the west, was originally houses for workers at the Stimson mill. Wallingford, as its name implies, was designed to set a somewhat different tone, one more like residential Brooklyn, the townlet that eventually became the University District—more middle than working class. Its proximity to the University, and its facing Lake Union and downtown, over time probably contributed to an assured tone, not the least cosmopolitan, but not uncultivated either.

North 45th, which has almost all of Wallingford's commerce, between Woodlawn on the west and Sunnyside on the east, is my candidate for the greatest ordinary street in Seattle. You can walk up one side and down the other in less than an hour. Since this *is* ordinary stuff, you can get little feel for it driving, especially since traffic is a steady stream and you can make no friends driving slowly.

When I tried once before to write about North 45th, a friend reported that while I might be right, what I had actually written was mostly a list of building establishments, something that the Wallingford Community Council might hand out. So, no lists. I know that when I am on a great ordinary street in some other city I enjoy myself without really caring about this or that store. On neighborhood streets, most of the people are residents, which is what sets North 45th off from Broadway or from The Ave in the University District. The providers of daily goods and services are not all franchises, especially not national or international ones like Radio Shack or McDonald's. On North 45th the supermarket is part of a four-store operation and has been there forever, the drugstore's chain does not extend beyond the county, Dick's (famous for fries) and ethnic restaurants provide the fast food, the dry cleaner is one of a kind, and the neighborhood movie house is part of a chain, but mostly of other neighborhood houses making people glad they're still open. The diner across from the movies is slightly more of a restaurant than a true diner, but only slightly. With the Wallingford Center, we have the only rival of Val Thomas's remodeled West Queen Anne Elementary for best redone school. Here, admittedly, you do real shopping, and you sit outside with your bagel and latte. But Wallingford accommodates itself to this tone rather than lets it set a tone for the rest. That's done by the Food Giant across the street.

If the criteria are materials used both lovingly and usefully, and the same language spoken differently and harmoniously, then residential Wallingford is Seattle's peaceable kingdom. You can find something similar in neighborhoods developed about the same time elsewhere in Seattle, but what they do in parts, Wallingford does throughout—or almost. You have taken my advice and shown your visitor Capitol Hill houses, which have been duly admired. Your visitor, seeing that Capitol Hill is Camelot, asks where do the simple folk live.

At this point this chapter ceases to be armchair reading; you have to go to North 40th and Burke Avenue North and start walking. If you were dutiful, you would go up Burke to 45th, down Meridian to 40th, back up on Bagley, down on Corliss, up on Sunnyside across 45th and up to the Good Shepherd Center, across to Wallingford Avenue, and back down to 40th. Yes, I know, no one takes a visitor on such a walk, since it is all too ordinary, all too much of a sameness. So let us try to get the principle of the thing.

At 4032 Burke is a house that is having a conversation with itself, in windows, rooflines, eaves, gables, song and echo. If you go east two blocks, on the southeast corner of 41st and Bagley is 4034, where the conversation is quieter, but parts are always aware of parts. This house, though, is at the north end of a sequence of five houses. Stand in the middle of the street to see all five. Despite the presence of a tree and a fence at 4018, you can see that it and 4028 are close to identical, and working with

4032 Burke, a house having a conversation with itself

41st and Bagley, moving south

the same speaking terms you noted on 4034. In between, 4024 and 4020 are different, modestly so, and the row exists as a row of friends. I once attended a wedding rehearsal lunch at 41st and Bagley. There were out-of-town visitors. They had seen the Market, the Needle, the Arboretum—now what? (It's usually a trip out of town.) I tried to say what I liked about the houses down the street, and why they were so much "Seattle," a city of houses whose major building material is wood. They listened, and nodded so dutifully I advised them to go to Broadway that night.

Now go back to Meridian and look at 4011, 4013, and 4017. Like what we have just been looking at, these are essentially teens and twenties houses—eaves, porches, dormers, roofs. But these I call Serbia, Bosnia, and Croatia, where the vocabulary is scrambled, the relations are antagonistic, and done without the intrusion of what usually makes for discord in the peaceable kingdom, namely either pretension or 1950s-1960s suburban.

Now, as to pretension, there is an interesting grouping of houses farther up Burke, where grandness keeps seeping in the farther you go. On the corner, 4235, its lower half brick, tries to stand out, and does, like a sore thumb. Two doors south, 4217, every bit as ambitious in its large Capitol Hill way, does not stick out in the bad sense, because it shares a setback and a porch line with its neighbor to the north. Get on some speaking terms and you will not be the cheese that stands alone.

The simple folk, though, do not live on Burke in these blocks. Walk, then, do not run, down to 42nd and Sunnyside. On the southeast corner, once again, is an attractive house, 4138, which plays a game with the roof eave and the porch eave. The next five houses to the south—and these are, neighborhood value aside, as plain and inexpensive as any in Seattle—play similar games with similar elements, and the game dominates the look of the houses. Keeping on, you have three that play with roofline

Bosnia, Croatia, and Serbia

and the window under it. Finally, on the corner, there's a house that looks like an unintentionally designed bookend for the house you started with, its rooflines on the right of the house, just as those of 4138 are on the left. You can have as much fun with these Sunnyside houses as with any sequence in the city; it's a pity that when trees are in leaf you can never take in the group as a group. Such designs do all that house designs can do to make people in love and charity with their neighbor.

Since Wallingford lots are small, this is not a great area for trees, so you will have to go slightly outside its prescribed limits, to 4625 Eastern, to see what amounts to a mini-arboretum, a huge Sierra redwood out front, and, amid the dense growth on either side, there's a dove tree to the south, a redbud to the north. But if you cannot identify these, you will see a yard planted as Highgate planted its cemetery in London—densely, wantonly. For the opposite effect, note the single deodar cedar on the west side of the Wallingford Center.

Nor need you be content with small lots. On the southwest corner of 62nd and Corliss, and on the northwest corner of 41st and Corliss, are large houses—mansions let us call them—on big lots, whose original buildings look like they go back into the nineteenth century. The bow window of the 41st and Corliss mansion is especially nice, three sided rather than the more usual semicircle.

Finally, we have 4311, 4313, 4315 Sunnyside, recently built, part of the 1970s and 1980s way with decently priced new houses on relatively small lots. On residential streets, especially in the Central Area, are many attempts to build new houses that blend easily with their neighbors. Here, though, the builder wanted garages as part of each house. That effectively set these off from houses to their north, which in turn necessitated excellent conversation among the three new ones. Above each garage are identical shapes and two porches, which seemed enough for the common language. The windows are slightly different in number and placement, and there are different rooflines, different stains for wood. The gradually receding setbacks go north to south, and it is do re mi.

NORTH LAKE UNION

Walk: an hour or a little more.
Bus: #70, 71, 72, 73, 74, 83, from Third and Union to the University District; #71, 72, 73 also run weekday expresses from the tunnel.

Walk south on any street below North 45th in Wallingford and you are aware of Lake Union at the bottom, and downtown beyond; this is one of the areas where the postmodern Washington Mutual and Two Union Square stand out. This walk is designed to make Lake Union something other than a backdrop. It is Seattle's working lake; and even its main leisure activity, boating, takes business forms here: marinas, marine supply, repairs, and sales, along with fish and seafood packers. To get a feel for this you need to stick as close to the shore as the fences allow you, bearing in mind that if the traffic here, or the close-up-ness of it, begins to make it seem unpleasant or pointless, you can cross the street and climb a few feet to the Burke-Gilman Trail. As you walk, try to concentrate on what's close up. The scene is interesting, it keeps changing, and at the end is Gas Works Park, which gives you one of Seattle's best views.

From many places in the University District, where the bus will take you, you can see the I-5 Ship Canal Bridge. You want to start underneath it next to the water, and there are plenty of parking places nearby. The freeway, including its express lanes, is directly above you, and making plenty of noise, so I doubt if picnic tables were a good idea here, but you can walk right down to the water and get your bearings. Portage Bay is to your left, Lake Union to your right. If you want to sit and look, better is the next water overlook, the barge outside Ivar's Salmon House. The food isn't much there, but you can pick up something cheap at the take-out window. Or keep going. Glimpse-outs and lookouts keep popping up, on the empty site of what once was Seattle Redi-Mix, by the Skansonia Ferry, a restaurant currently called Thieves Rib & Ale House, in a tree-covered area between two marinas. Whenever the weather is good and people want to be outdoors, the area here, at water's edge and on the lake, is full of activity. If you yourself are a boat person, or like to hear boat talk, you might go up and down the dock of a marina as if your boat were here, or stop in at the JD Company supply store.

Just past a sign that reads Gasworks Park Marina Condominium, a gravel path bends away from Northlake Way toward the water. You will see a scoop law sign, two bird houses on long poles, then a large multitrunked white poplar and two picture perfect willows. This is the unannounced beginning of Gas Works Park.

The great parks created in Seattle's first flowering were essentially preserved wilderness; those of the second flowering, in the 1970s and 1980s, had to be made from land previously used, and of these Gas Works is the jewel. Richard Haag's genius is expressed here in two ways: put the large mound in the middle (the mounds in Victor Steinbrueck Park are his too), and leave the rest alone. When the paved path turns here, leave it and cleave to the water's edge. Most times of most days, it will be you and the geese here, maybe an otherwise homeless person making a home. There are two building complexes on your right, the first full of Ingersoll Rand machines, the second the great abandoned gas works itself. In defiance of the barbed wire fence that tries to

Gas Works, the jewel of the recycled parks of the 1970s

keep folks out but manages only to invite youth in, the likes of "MAMA TROLL" and "I Love You Heather" are painted on the gas works. It's hard to say if this structure was always beautiful, since it was built to be strictly functional and is in some ways ugly, but especially on cloudy, windy days you can walk around and find it hard to keep your eyes from tracing the intricacies of its shapes and the power of its outline against the sky.

At least as impressive as the gas works is the view. The other great view of downtown from over water, at Duwamish Head, feels quite different. There, if you come to it via the laid back, away-feeling Alki Beach, you're *confronted* with the great towers. Here you have been making your way among urban business, and then the scene opens out and the urban is now at a distance, framed by Capitol and Queen Anne hills, and you control the view more than it does you. The blue-green late 1980s skyscrapers stand out, dull in winter when the lake is slate gray, bright on sunny days in warm months when the lake is almost blue. So, after you pick out these behemoths, name as many downtown, Regrade, Queen Anne, and Capitol Hill buildings as you can. The view is best, I think, when you take the walk from urban-near to urban-far, but Gas Works is a fine short walk by itself. The hill is excellent for flying kites (kite stores can be found in the shopping area between Northlake Way and North 34th), for picnics, for watching summer sunsets behind Aurora Bridge, for Fourth of July fireworks, for a sunrise service Easter morning.

To return to the I-5 bridge: The Burke-Gilman Trail begins just northeast of Gas Works Park. This keeps you away from cars but puts you in the path of bikers, and because the trail is on a railbed, its rights-of-way on either side insulate you from the surroundings. Or you can wend your way back on residential Wallingford streets.

11 University District and University of Washington

The former is called the U District, or just the District, and its main street, University Way N.E., is called The Ave. When the University of Washington, called U Dub, or the U, moved to its present campus in 1895, University Bridge had already been built and a streetcar ran out from downtown to the small community of Brooklyn and to the even smaller one of Ravenna. Brooklyn remains in name only, as the street one block west of The Ave. In a 1902 photograph, when there were three buildings on the University campus, Brooklyn had about a hundred houses.

As the University grew, Brooklyn became the University District. It took on apartments, established commerce on The Ave, and moved north to merge with Ravenna and west to merge with Wallingford. For a long time, clearly, though it accommodated the university students, it was its own neighborhood, and people lived and worked there who had no university ties. This could not last. When Mark Tobey was living in the District in 1950, he said: "This house is better suited for the operation of a hit-and-miss cleaning shop, or a drive-in boiler factory, than it is to the artist." Tobey soon left, and his house is currently home for

Outrageous Taco, one of the few frame dwellings left south of 45th. All this took place before the huge expansion of the University—more than doubling its size in the 1965–75 decade to its current 33,000 to 35,000 students—changed things forever. Commerce pushed out into what had been residential areas, and shifted its orientation away from the neighborhood and toward the students.

This means that the relation of the University to its surroundings is virtually seamless. A private university like Columbia or the University of Chicago can isolate itself within the city, but public ones cannot, and this one does not want to. Its appetite for nearby land seems boundless, so it, like the expanding commerce, makes the District less and less a place for people to live. But one good reason for the University to expand outward is its desire not to change the essential character of the campus by building upward.

The Ave is one of the liveliest streets in Seattle, and is well worth your walking from as far south as N.E. 40th up to N.E. 55th. The street's character changes slightly about every five blocks. It is like Broadway in a host of ways: businesses tend toward fast food and inexpensive ethnic restaurants; it can't support an ambitious restaurant; it changes so often it is hard to remember how many stores—House of Rice, La Tienda, Shiga's, Johnny's Flower Shop, Varsity Theatre, University Book Store, Porter and Jensen, Costas—have been there close to forever; it attracts lots of people who come to hang out because the place itself is a scene; it doesn't sell much you couldn't buy elsewhere. Alas, unlike Broadway, it shuts down at night, and when it does it can seem anything from unsavory to ominous and, occasionally, worse.

The Ave also has a major visitor attraction, of a magnitude greater than any single thing on Broadway: the University Book Store. Outside and in, it has close to zero charm; on another street its brutal façade would hurt more than it does here, where no one notices buildings. Inside, too much of the available space is given over to things that aren't books, and the aisles often are so cramped it does not feel like a good place to browse when it gets close to busy. So treat the place like a supermarket, and you will find it a superb supermarket. It may not be as good with literature as Elliott Bay in Pioneer Square, but its range may be wider and its depth within the academic disciplines of arts and sciences greater.

The walk I propose of part of the University of Washington campus begins at its north entrance, N.E. 45th and 17th N.E. If you stand at this juncture and face away from the campus and look up 17th, you will see Greek Row, made notable by its street trees, mostly horse chestnuts, making a canopy over the pavement. Since there is no ideal place to consider the park-and-boulevard system that is the major legacy of old residential Seattle, some words can be said about it here.

The names usually associated with it are the Olmsted Brothers, sons of the great Frederick Law Olmsted, most famous for his design of New York's Central Park. In the first decade of this century, the Olmsted Brothers, especially J. C. and Frederick Dawson, were hired to design the grounds for the Alaska-Yukon-Pacific Exposition and to lay out The Highlands, then and now the area's most prestigious residential enclave, and parts of the newly developed Mount Baker neighborhood. Most of all, a boulevard system was desired that would connect the park land the city had been busily acquiring, starting with Washington Park (the Arboretum) in 1900 and culminating with the acquisition of Bailey Peninsula, which became Seward Park in 1911. A lot of other people were involved in these projects, most notably J. J. McGilvra, the squire of Madison Park, the father-in-law of Thomas Burke, and the president of the Parks Board in these years. But the Olmsted name is the one that has stuck, and rightly so.

Lake Washington Boulevard begins at Seward Park to the south, and ends at Montlake Boulevard just south of the University of Washington campus; it will be considered in various chapters to come. Rainier Vista, the spine of the campus, the major legacy of the A-Y-P Exposition, is the "boulevard" on campus. North of the campus is Greek Row, on 17th N.E., leading to Ravenna Boulevard, a wide street with a median that begins at one end of Ravenna Park and makes its way west to Green Lake, at the far end of which is Woodland Park. All this was part of the Olmsted Plan. They also designed roads that would continue on from Seward Park on the south and climb Beacon Hill to Jefferson Park, and on from Woodland Park to the west to Fort Lawton (now Discovery Park) overlooking Puget Sound in Magnolia, but these never came to be.

One way to say what the Olmsted's boulevards were doing was going where streetcars did not. Their employers were, literally, the carriage trade—soon to become the automobile trade. Streetcars, for instance, ran out Madison Street to Madison Park on Lake Washington, which the splendid haughty H. A. Chadwick, for years editor of *The Argus,* a glossy weekly, called "a playground for the Industrials, a breathing spot for the Employed. . . . of the people, for the people, by the people. . . . But you don't see family parties there to spend a quiet day out of doors, nor mothers with nervous children, nor society girls with their fiancees." That catches the tone perfectly; the houses, streets, and neighborhoods that were built around the boulevards, and away from the streetcars as much as possible, were not for "the Industrials" or "the Employed."

Of course the buses that are the heirs of the streetcars, and the cars that are heirs to the carriages, now go to almost every spot on the park/boulevard system. Thus what was not then by the people is now of the people and for the people. But the boulevard system remains as it was: a beautiful landscape, manufactured as little as possible, never showy, open but not wild, civilized without being urban. To this day the only places of commerce in the entire system are a spot near Leschi Park and another at the east side of Green Lake.

And their tone is that of the older parts of the University campus as well.

Walk: an hour and a half.
Bus: #70, 71, 72, 73, 74, 83, from Third and Union; #71, 72, 73 also run weekday expresses from the tunnel. Get off at N.E. 45th and walk east uphill.

A Connecticut friend of mine once said, "All college campuses look good," by which he meant that all campuses to which any child of his might be sent look good. They do, and they are in the East, the Midwest, and the South. Large university campuses in the West, however, more often than not do not look good and some are as forbidding as hospitals.

The University of Washington campus has some terrible things, and on a scale that makes blunders elsewhere seem minor, but it is a fine place, one of the top ten attractions in Seattle. The University has been at its present site since 1895; its first building was Denny Hall, named for Arthur Denny, Seattle's leading pioneer, and built like its downtown predecessor, on a knoll, not far from the University's northern border. Shortly thereafter came Lewis and Clark halls, and a tiny observatory. This was ample for the few hundred college-level students enrolled at the turn of the century. Most of the buildings on the campus erected for the A-Y-P Exposition were temporary, but Rainier Vista was created then. It was framed, in the 1920s by Suzzallo Library and after World War II by the Administration Building.

Bebb & Gould became the University's architect in 1915, and Carl Gould had a hand in designing most of its buildings between then and World War II. Gould had the same kind of quiet elegance that is the hallmark of his contemporary, and perhaps the University's greatest professor, Vernon Louis Parrington, though Gould was to the manor born as Parrington was not. It is fortunate Gould did as much as he did because in the forty years after World War II, the period of the University's greatest expansion, almost everything that was built was bad—bland, ugly, brutal—with the dormitories and the Health Sciences complex constantly vying to see who could be worst. (There are exceptions, and we will see some of them.) A great many of the newer buildings, unpleasant to look at from the outside, are also discouraging inside—in many places helping to deaden relations, between teachers and students, and among students.

Then, at the end of it all, came Edward Larrabee Barnes's Allen Library, completed in 1991, which may be the UW's finest building and certainly is its best for many years. It gives the campus a focal point that is not primarily a matter of natural beauty, and it even can suggest that the major reason for the University to exist is to nurture the life of the mind.

From your starting point at N.E. 45th and 17th N.E., first note on your left one of the oldest and smallest buildings on campus, the Observatory, which celebrated its centennial in 1992. Stargazing will never supplant gardening or birding in Seattle, but the Observatory is open to the public Monday and Thursday nights, 7–9 in winter, 9–11 in summer, slide shows on cloudy nights. Your next move is to stop at the campus gate and pick up a map from its guardian.

The road here is Memorial Way, lined by twenty-five rows of

University of Washington Observatory

London plane trees (in American, sycamore), four to the row, to honor UW men and women killed in World War I. It is gorgeous and hushing, and as a bonus here you get the trunks of two very tall firs that do not branch until they are taller than the planes. The walk begins here, incidentally, not just because it is the most striking of the three entrances, but also to stress that most of what is endearing about the campus is out of doors, as available to the visitor as much as to those who work and live here. Sometimes it is architecture, sometimes trees and shrubs, always there is a good sense of things being well kept up. Thus, on your left as you go down Memorial Way is Denny Hall, which has high-ceilinged, light, airy classrooms, with movable chairs and blackboards wherever there are no windows. But you want to stay outdoors and go right, around the back of Parrington Hall. At the far end of the lawn here, to the north, in addition to two rare shingle oaks, is a stand of madrona trees that seemed doomed a decade ago but are doing better since the grass beneath them is no longer mowed.

Go around the west side of Parrington, cross the road, go down the steps between two brick buildings. On either side of the flagpole, amid rhododendrons, is a shrub planting of Euonymus *alata,* nice in leaf, blazing red in autumn, and showing a brilliant branch structure in winter. You then emerge onto Red Square (officially Central Plaza), the brainchild of then President Charles Odegaard in the late 1960s. The undergraduate library, on your right, is named for him, and since its acronym is OUGL, it is called the Ugly. My hunch is that Odegaard much admired the plaza Fred Bassetti designed between Loew Hall and the Engineering Library, and said to himself, "If some's good, more's better." It isn't, and Red Square is a wasteland, slippery and dangerous when wet, which is half the year, fit only for skateboarders, a menace to themselves and others. Camellias that had graced the front of the Administration Building were taken out and red oaks were inexplicably put in. Nor are the other structures of the same time—Kane Hall on your left, the broken obelisk, the Ugly, or Meany Hall beyond the Ugly—much to look at, though Meany is an excellent theater and concert hall.

What Red Square could not destroy was Gould's Suzzallo Library (mid-1920s) and the Administration Building (late 1940s). Of these two buildings, the one thing you should not miss is the Graduate Reading Room in the Library. Go in the entrance facing you and up the stairs on the right. This is Gould's one attempt at grandeur in the library; it seems entirely successful as a design, though rather intimidating as a reading room. It is really good for concerts, and it is a pity it is not thus used more often.

Back outside. Rainier Vista is best seen standing between Suzzallo and the Administration Building, when Mount Rainier is out, Drumheller Fountain is on, the roses are in bloom, and Frosh Pond is filled with ducks. Its pinnacle day, though, comes only a few times a year at most: midwinter, rosebushes bare, fountain quiet, geese and not ducks dominant, the mountain fully covered with snow and looking to be ten rather than a hundred miles away. A few years ago, when Health Sciences was building an underground parking lot at the far end of the vista, and the question was what should go on top, it was said that Rainier Vista might be the best single viewing spot in the Northwest. It certainly has a claim to be one of the best *designed* viewpoints. The best place to see Rainier, though, is at Tipsoo Lake on U.S. 410 going up to Chinook Pass, where you see the mountain and its reflection in the lake. But I have never been on Rainier Vista without feeling, however briefly, some raising of the spirit.

Down the steps, Physics on the left, Johnson on the right, both serviceable buildings enhanced by their location; then, set back

Memorial Way, University of Washington

some, Guggenheim on the left and Bagley on the right. Past these, on either side of the vista path, are trees, and markedly contrasting spaces. On the right is the Medicinal Herb Garden, where every one of hundreds of specimens of trees, shrubs, and herbs is labeled. Plants are jammed next to plants, the walkways are narrow, everything feels squnched in, hidden even, so you always seem to be seeing something that was not there last time. Of the trees I especially like the pair of golden yews in the middle, and the smoke tree on the north border—you have to see it in late spring, after flowering, to understand its name. Then, on the other side of the vista walk is the Sylvan Theater, as open as the Herb Garden is crowded. The pillars were brought here when the original downtown University building was razed, and the trees are superb. This is the best place on campus for a picnic, a tryst, a nap, or a long long thought.

After the Sylvan Theater, continue to swing east and north on Stevens Way. To your right is a bust, and before discovering whose face it is, quiz yourself thus: if there are only three outdoor statues on the campus, all put up within the lifetimes of its first college graduates, and all with names known to people who have no knowledge of the University's history, of whom would they be? George Washington, yes—he's on the other side of Meany Hall, facing the sunset. The one here is James J. Hill, founder of the Great Northern Railroad, robber baron without peer, whose decision to establish Seattle as his train's western terminus has been alleged to be the making of the city, and is certainly responsible for his bust being here. The third, to be found in the grove between the Library and Thomson Hall, is Edvard Grieg, presumably because he was Scandinavian like so many late nineteenth-century immigrants to Seattle, and not infamous like Ibsen or Strindberg. The choices seem expressive and naive, and I like it that the University never tried to cover its traces by adding to these three.

Hill's bust is in the midst of uninteresting engineering buildings, except for the aforementioned plaza by Bassetti, on your right as you come up Stevens Way. If you are here during term time, especially at the half hour, when classes change, you may see a nice contrast. In the plaza, people respond to its implicit friendliness by lingering, to talk, read, and smoke; across the street they wait for buses, stone-faced and grim, ignoring the fine row of hornbeams lining the roadway.

The bus stop is at the back end of the HUB (Student Union Building), and to your right if you go in the entrance here is an espresso bar.

Go around the HUB to the left and face west. Across the greensward is the University's new gem, the Allen Library. I urge you to take some time with it; inside it is mostly a nice place for books to be housed and read, in need of things on its walls, but outside it is a wonder. First, the landscaping. Though some species trees were removed to build the library, the giant Atlas cedar is now exposed as never before, and it is a great ungainly beast. The open space is now so occupied by the prospect that there actually seems to be more green space than there was before the library was built. Then notice the effect of this building on those near it. Nothing could be done to hide the ugliness of the diamonded Sieg Hall to the south, but the all-glass addition to Suzzallo is now muted and harder to see than heretofore. The Allen has a number of different brick patterns, and you find yourself, as you walk around, comparing them with those on Physics, Suzzallo, Smith, the HUB. In fact, no pattern is repeated, but it is fun to find that out, and to note what is in effect a lavish series of themes and variations in brick.

Edward Larrabee Barnes's Allen Library, solemnly playing at a cathedral

Edward Larrabee Barnes's way with University Gothic is a far cry from Carl Gould's, but the two do not clash. Look at Allen from the HUB and you can see many elements of a cathedral: nave to the left, altar to the right, "rose window" in the middle above, except it is not a rose nor is its glass stained; a rose window nonetheless. So too an "arch" that doesn't arch but everyone rightly calls it one. This keeps the building from having a front, back, and sides; all sides serve as fronts. Seen from the HUB, the arch looks like it must be a front door, but when you go to it you see it is only a walkway. Move over to the low brick wall that goes from Allen to Thomson, and now the arch is hidden and the "side" entrance is the "front"; go to the west side and you have no sense that you are at the rear of the building.

Finally, walk under the arch. There is nothing to it, since it is only a walkway, but the space feels important, the secular counterpart of holy. Barnes plays with his materials—as was de rigueur in the late 1980s—but the effect of this place is stilling; not awe, because that would be more than is wanted, but stilling. No skateboards here. Before Allen the University publicity people had to use Rainier Vista or Gould's quadrangle with the Yoshino cherries in bloom as the campus's signature spaces, and now they need not.

Keep in mind as much as you can of Barnes's ways and means and make your way to the quadrangle, but unhurriedly, since to gain its full effect you must come at it from the east. Go from the front of the HUB through the parking lot to the north, pause by the gorgeous "Pink Beauty" crabapple at the southeast corner of Communications, cross the street at the three-way stop to sit on the bench and enjoy a fine city-water-mountain view, re-cross the street to pass between the aged, deep red brick of Clark and Lewis halls, turn left and walk between Art and Music.

It is best when the cherries are in bloom, to be sure, but in all seasons the trees, now gnarly and imposing, help make this a fine scene. On all the buildings the signature Gothic feature is the arch, especially on Smith, Savery, Raitt, and Miller. The arch is on the second floor, a staircase leads up to it, and the arches are echoed in the window and roofline decorations. Gould has placed all this into a severely designed classic symmetrically arranged space, so that steps face steps, rooflines match, walkways make squares and rectangles, the cherries are in neat rows. Overall the scene is as much like Christopher Wren's Greenwich as it is like Princeton Gothic.

If you exit the quadrangle via the north, spend a minute or two with some massive maples, whose branches are as big as the trunks of many maples, elms, and oaks, all of which nicely keep Denny Hall from being fully exposed. Then, back up Memorial Way, across from the Observatory, is the Burke Museum, not a handsome building, but its collection of Northwest Native American art and artifacts is perhaps the best reason on the entire campus for a visitor to go indoors. Unless it is for coffee and pastry at the Boiserie, which you get to via the parking lot at the south end of the Burke.

This does not exhaust the interest of the campus, though I think it gets most of it. One of its best known structures is Husky Stadium, essentially the work of George Wellington Stoddard in 1948, Z-shaped and impressive, best seen on one of the Arboretum walks described in the next chapter. Two other highlights can be taken in while walking The Ave: the Henry Gallery, which borders 15th Avenue N.E., and which is host to some good traveling exhibitions, and the Friendship Grove, a large, unobtrusive collection of trees on Campus Parkway, each tree labeled and identified with a foreign country. Then, at the southeast extremity of the campus, beyond Husky Stadium, is the Waterfront Activities Center (if this were not an academic institution, it would just be a boathouse), where you can rent a canoe or rowboat and explore the waters and marshy shorelines of Union Bay.

The best of the University of Washington is the look of the place, which includes the way students and faculty are part of, as well as apart from, Seattle. Part of, because most of them live and work in the city; apart from, because the dress and the tone is different from, say, both Fourth Avenue downtown and Woodland Park Zoo.

Of course the dress and tone are not different from what is found on most college and university campuses, but every time I have been away from it for a while, and return to see it some-what freshly, I am aware of an earnestness, an intentness. Since it does not necessarily include humor, it can sometimes be pompous or solemn, in response to which, the younger ones might nod obediently, or be noisy. Since what creates the tone is the effect people have on each other, I could wish that more of those who live and work on the campus could see it for the frequently beautiful place it is. You will have no difficulty in that respect.

12 Arboretum

S eattle's Parks and Recreation Department calls it "Washington Park Arboretum," while the College of Forest Resources and the Center for Urban Horticulture of the University of Washington call it "University of Washington Arboretum in Washington Park." And thereby hangs a tale, a history, and a tension genuine enough that I propose two walks, one taken in "Washington Park Arboretum," the other in "UW Arboretum in Washington Park." Each has a different route, and a different person taking them, though each is you.

Much of the 200 acres was originally owned by the Puget Mill Company, the local arm of the San Francisco lumber giant Pope and Talbot. After they logged it off, they sold the land to the city (holding onto larger parcels to the east which later became Broadmoor). In 1904, Lake Washington Boulevard was built through it as part of the Olmsteds' system. The current arboretum's main walk, Azalea Way, was first a race course for the gentle folk who were the Olmsteds' patrons.

The University established an arboretum on its campus as part of the A-Y-P Exposition of 1909; it was not moved to its present location until 1934. The Parks Department administered the land from the beginning, and continues to do so, while the University cares for everything that grows on it. Thus, if you wonder why drainage on Azalea Way is a perpetual problem, ask the Parks Department; when you find no identifying number on a tree that is unfamiliar to you, curse the University. Of course, if it is the traffic on the Boulevard you mind, blame the Olmsteds.

The Parks Department no doubt finds its problems are mostly those it has with all its better loved places, but the University's horticulturists are perpetually feeling compromised by having the arboretum be a park. Here is Arthur Lee Jacobson in *Trees of Seattle:* "The *location* of our arboretum is, to phrase it as politely as possible, a mixed blessing with more bitterness than the recipe calls for. On the whole it is too low, wet, cold, shady and poorly drained.... Our arboretum was intended to grow trees in conditions more or less like those found in undisturbed nature.... [The chief problem with that is] the subtle, gradual suppression of many non-native plantings by the better-adapted wild natives. Where the average old-fashioned arboretum shows open-grown oaks exulting in their own peculiar shapes, our arboretum is growing a forest of tall, slender oak trunks fighting each other for sunlight and space. It is obviously a mistake to exclude peach trees and spreading live oaks because there is an overabundance of mediocre native firs, cedars, maples and alders. But that is what is happening."

You, of course, are not required to find the native trees "mediocre," and some are as old as the century. It is true, however, that any attempt by the University's people to remove bigleaf maples and Douglas firs to make room for something more exotic would be greeted with alarm by most of the public, who like the plantings but also like to feel the paths are cutting through wildness.

Walk 1: two and one-half hours.

Bus: #43 to 24th Avenue East and Boyer Avenue East, then walk east on Boyer to Lake Washington Boulevard, and along the boulevard and right to the first parking lot.

For a jog at dawn, for a leisurely walk with a friend, for a place to show off arrays of colors to a visitor during Seattle's long springs and falls, as a place to make love after dark in warm weather, Washington Park is one of the premier places in the city. This walk starts at the only parking lot on the Arboretum side of Lake Washington Boulevard. Start by crossing the street and going through the Japanese Tea Garden (nominal fee), where the art is bonsai and everything is designed to be graceful and ornamental rather than strong or wild. You might call ahead (the number is listed under City Parks in front white pages) to learn when tea ceremonies are performed; infrequently but worth it.

When done here, come back across the boulevard and you'll find Azalea Way cutting off north by northeast, starting at a very nice red horse chestnut. Azalea Way is at its best, perhaps, when the deciduous azaleas are in bloom, but the track is lined with flowering cherries, which start blooming in February, and the fall color throughout the Arboretum is splendid. Jogging and cycling are not allowed here—you can jog on the bare paths and cycle on the paved roads—so the pace is slow and pleasant. Save forays up the valleys into the woods for later.

At the far end of Azalea Way, across Arboretum Drive, is the Visitor Center. Stop in, to get a map of the area, to buy a post-card, or get information about a plant for which you found no identifying tag. Then continue on heading down the slope toward the water, bearing right and passing some gnarly old willows. Over the bridge, you're on Foster Island, which has not only hundreds of birches and alders, but a freeway running through it. Though the trees are hardly a jungle, they muffle automobile

Washington Park Arboretum, north end, near Union Bay

165 ARBORETUM

noise quite well from fifty yards away. Pass under the freeway, then just before you get to the northern end of the island, hang a left and you'll be on a marsh trail.

A remarkable scene, this. In 1917, when the locks were opened, the marsh was created when fresh water, about 20 feet above sea level, flowed into Puget Sound. You'll hear more birds than you'll see, and most of what you'll see is in glimpses, rustlings in the reeds. There will be canoes, yachts, sailboats, and barges on Union Bay during all but the stormiest daylight hours. Across the bay the main object in view is Husky Stadium. Off to the northeast are the affluent homes of Webster Point and Laurelhurst. In between, where marsh once extended inland for almost a mile, where later the city operated a dump, is mostly playing fields for half a dozen sports.

Standing in Gas Works Park, you know you are in a city; standing on the north end of Seward Park, you can see downtown skyscrapers but city feels far away. The scene here in the marsh is in between these two. Everything urban is at a distance, not far away, yet not markedly urban either; people dot this scene, few are working, or doing what you are doing. Let us call it suburban/urban, which is appropriate since the trail itself, Husky Stadium, and the Webster Point houses were all built in the 1950s and 1960s, when suburban/urban was considered the best thing to be.

The trail mostly ends when you hit mainland, though you can continue on and not stop until you are through the Montlake Cut a half mile to the west. You will be facing the Museum of History and Industry. Its regular exhibits probably are not worth your time, but it has good special shows occasionally, so you might inquire. Regardless, you are well away from the Arboretum by now, and you must find your way back. Try going around to the right of the museum and over the bridge across the freeway, across Lake Washington Boulevard, wind a little until you get to East Roanoke, left until you get to 26th, right until you find yourself at a children's play area, at the far end of which is a path. This will lead you over the boulevard by a footbridge—on your right is an enormous stately white poplar—and back into the Arboretum proper. Soon on either side of you are various nonnative oaks, which are suffering the equivalent of animals being in cages in a zoo. Most are tagged and can be spotted easily.

You are soon back onto Azalea Way. Turn right. In late fall and winter, go left at the Woodland Garden, then left again at the top into the Winter Garden, a breathtaking place when the witch-hazels are in bloom. In the spring, skip Woodland Garden and go up into the next left, Loderi Valley, to see a dazzling display of hybrid rhododendrons. Whatever the season, go south along the winding trails that are roughly parallel to Azalea Way. Any route is good woodland, the cedars especially are majestic, and you will see what a task the Arboretum people would face if they attempted to replace the native trees on a scale large enough to give full room to nonnative exotics. Down the hill to your right is the parking lot that was your point of origin.

(For bus riders, a variation. Go up Loderi Valley or Woodland Garden on your outward journey, so you can declare your walk over when you get to the Museum of History and Industry, at which point you can turn right on Lake Washington Boulevard and catch a #43 back downtown from Montlake Boulevard.)

Walk 2: three hours.
Bus: #11 from Third and Pike. Alight at East Madison and Lake Washington Boulevard. Go north on the boulevard down a marvelous canopy of oaks and plane trees, turn right at Arboretum Drive, walk uphill and start your walk just past the first parking area.

For this walk you should be alone, and use as your companion either *Woody Plants in the University of Washington Arboretum* or Jacobson's *Trees of Seattle,* both of which are on sale at the Visitor Center; failing either of those, this book will do.

Starting from the first parking turnout on Arboretum Drive, your aim here is to walk mostly on the outer edge of the Arboretum proper. Even on weekend afternoons, you will probably find yourself alone most of the time. Go slowly, look at all the identification tags, though those in metal give only Latin names; all tags have a number, the last two digits of which, after the dash, indicate the year the tree was planted.

The point about the tags is instructive. With few exceptions they are for trees and shrubs planted by the Arboretum people, and consist of nonnatives, and plants in special collections. Since there are so many native trees here—not specimens, but trees— more are unmarked than marked. If you find no tag on a tree, you may feel you "should know it," and if you don't you should be chatting with a friend on Azalea Way. Fight this impulse. If you are feeling intrepid, take a leaf from a tree you cannot identify to the Visitor Center, and do not flinch if you are told it is a maple, but a dwarf maple; a cedar, but a deodar cedar. The aim of this walk is not to have you play expert, but to look at trees as hard as you can and have fun.

From the turnout keep to a path that usually runs parallel to the fence; Broadmoor golf course is on the other side. Soon you are in a collection of *Hamamelis,* or witch-hazel (I use Latin names in places where that is all the tags say), a quite nondescript tree when not in bloom. Soon after, you are in a group of trees related at least in appearance: epaulettes (*Pterostyrax*), silverbells (*Halesia*), and snowbells (*Styrax*). There is a large multitrunked epaulette near the fence, but mostly these are small trees, excellent for standing under and looking up. It is worth noting that the leaves of one species of snowbell bear no resemblance to those of another, which plays hell with any attempt you make to learn to identify them. Keep remembering that the varieties of oak are so different the only thing they have in common is acorns.

The largest snowbell is just before the next parking turnout; the smallest was planted in 1986 and has a long way to go to catch up; it is in the bed above the turnout. Almost directly across Arboretum Drive from it is a large sourwood, one of the showiest of all trees in its fall color, a crimson Seattle has too little of. There is also a stripebark maple against the fence here, but it is hard to get to or to see well. Best keep to the open area and come to a splendid grouping. The obvious stars are two "Sunburst" honey locusts (*Gleditsia* triacanthos) with their brilliant pale yellow leaves. Almost surrounding them, and continuing on, are black locusts (*Robinia pseudoacacia*), including a fine gnarly one by the fence, three very large ones together, and, at the end, some pink flowering hybrids. If, incidentally, you do not know a black locust but these are familiar, it may be because it is the feature tree in the African savanna at Woodland Park Zoo. It is a wonderfully airy and graceful tree. Nearby are two trees very rare to Seattle, a maackia and a yellow-wood, both distantly related to black locusts.

Past the locusts is a small but very impressive collection of redwoods, giant sequoias, the world's most massive trees. These particular trees are only fifty years old, but they were large twenty-five years ago, and here you can stand back and see them from a distance. If these youngsters survive, they will die sometime after 2300. How good are their chances?

Shortly after the redwoods comes one of the Arboretum's major collections, mountain ashes (*Sorbus*), in an almost bewildering variety, a number of which do not look, either in bark or leaf, like what is growing in your neighbor's yard. Almost all do not branch until they are well off the ground, which contributes to their air of massive strength, though in height and girth they are not "large" compared with our native conifers, poplars, and maples. Be on the lookout for the handsome *S. latifolia* or *devoniensis*.

Past the mountain ashes is the nursery, closed to the public, so you should cross Arboretum Drive here and see a fine yellow poplar, followed by a pretty grouping of Japanese red- and green-leaved maples serving as backdrop for a Carrière hawthorn, a tree broader than it is tall. Coming back to the east side you are soon in orchard, crabapples mostly, that to me are interesting only when flowering in April, utterly gorgeous then. Following the orchard you are in the parking lot of the Visitor Center, where you can buy a postcard or a book, find a toilet, or get a leaf identified. In the parking lot is a row of katsuras, a graceful tree that seems to be both common and generally unnoticed in Seattle.

Past the Visitor Center, go down to the water. In spring there are brilliant lavender flowers on two empress trees (*Paulownia tomentosa*), and the leaves are enormous. This time, go left, to the lindens, and stop under one of them. Lindens are limes in England, and Coleridge was immobilized under one in the summer of 1797:

> Nor in this bower,
> This little lime-tree bower, have I not mark'd
> Much that has sooth'd me. Pale beneath the blaze
> Hung the transparent foliage; and I watch'd
> Some broad and sunny leaf, and lov'd to see
> The shadow of the leaf and stem above
> Dappling its sunshine!

Coleridge was in "prison" under these limes because he had had an accident that prevented his walking with friends, but the tree itself can be prison, though the leaves are transparent and the sun can dapple them. Under the snowbells and silverbells earlier you could look up and delight in the tree covering like a parasol. Here the tree almost encases, and one concentrates on the leaves along the lower edges as they show shades of gray and green and pale green.

The lindens continue along the road to the far side of the next parking turnout. Cross the road into an area that ought to be one of the Arboretum's finest, filled as it is with oaks and beeches, but here especially Jacobson's complaint is true: there just is not enough room. For me, the worst of it is that across the boulevard here was a meadow that then became an urban vegetable garden P-patch, which then became Conifer Meadow. A perfect place to plant a few staggering oaks and beeches—why this? Maybe because the Pinetum to the south, on the west side of the boulevard, does not show its trees off well enough. Whatever. See what you can of the oaks and beeches; stay on this side of the road except for a foray onto the East Lynn Street bridge to see the enormous 100 foot white poplar next to the bridge.

Your aim now is to keep between Azalea Way and the boulevard, where there are a couple of paths and much to see. Japanese walnut and Texas walnut next to each other, then a serviceberry tree (*Amelanchier arborea*), much more beautiful than the shrubby serviceberries that are advertised on Azalea Way. A row of viburnums that are showy in spring, followed by a collection of true ashes (*Fraxinus*), relatives only of the *Sorbus* along Arboretum Drive. Past a bunch of alders, by the stream are two black cottonwoods, and then, slightly apart, a third, standing on its own, over 14 feet around, maybe the grandest deciduous tree in the Arboretum. Treat it like a skyscraper and walk around, at various distances, and promise never again to listen to anyone

telling you that poplars and cottonwoods are large weeds.

Past these giants, Azalea Way angles in on you and soon you'll come to its termination at the red horse chestnut. Any paths that will take you up and over the hill will do. I suggest: climb the hill to the grass path, turn right, then left uphill when the track becomes dirt, to the next dirt path. Left here past the light yellow-leaved *Euonymus japonicus* uphill to the similarly colored hollies, and you are back where you started. This is all native woodland, and if you are taking the bus and need no more of that, simply walk back up the boulevard to Madison and the #11.

If for me on this walk it is the silverbells and snowbells at the outset, the stretch with various locusts, followed by the redwoods and the mountain ashes, the lindens at the north end, the white poplar by the bridge, walnuts and a serviceberry leading to the cottonwoods, remember that the Arboretum has over 5,000 different specimens, so more than likely some things I have only carelessly glanced at will catch your eye. For me, the reward of treating the Arboretum as an arboretum, beyond the experience itself, is that it enriches my walks when I treat it as a park, to say nothing of my walks elsewhere in the city. For years I was a house watcher as I walked, trying to see how houses made the city. Doing the work for this book has taken away none of that, but now I add trees, especially trees when they are not flowering or showing fall color. The Arboretum shows as no other place in Seattle can how limited most people are when it comes to planting trees and shrubs. We must have more serviceberry trees.

University of Washington Arborteum in Washington Park: a black cottonwood; "in winter here no heart need mourn for summer or for spring"

13 Lake Washington Ridge: Madison Park to Mount Baker

The long ridge on the western slope of Lake Washington has no official name. It encompasses the neighborhoods of Madison Park, Washington Park, Denny Blaine, Madrona, Leschi, and Mount Baker, few of which have definite boundaries. I have heard it called the Gold Coast, and if the name will not do, I know of none better. Those who live to its immediate west, in the Central Area and Rainier Valley, think of it as something like a gold coast.

After the western slopes of First and Capitol hills and the south and western slopes of Queen Anne had been built on, the next generation reached for land above Lake Washington. Streetcar lines were built out Madison to Madison Beach, out Union to Madrona Beach, out Yesler to Leschi Park, and, a little later, out Jackson to a ferry terminal at Day Street. There are houses on the ridge that date from the 1890s, but 1900–1920 were the decisive decades because Lake Washington Boulevard was the decisive street; its carriage trade tone came to dominate, and even today, as you move south from the shopping area at Madison Park, only a clutch of stores at Leschi keeps it from being totally residential for the next ten miles. (For the creation of Lake Washington Boulevard, see the beginning of the section of Chapter 11 devoted to the University of Washington.)

Yet—if "yet" is the correct conjunction here—there is much of interest, plenty for two considerable walks.

Walk 1: about two hours.
Bus: #11 to the foot of East Madison.

Everything the residents of Pioneer Square wish they had in the way of commercial convenience Madison Park has: a good hardware store, a couple of pharmacies, a famously good school, a small supermarket with charge customers, wine shop, cheese shop, jeweler, all the necessary professional services. If you want to start this walk with refreshment, have coffee and pastry at Stoll's Madison Park Bakery; if you want to end it thus, have beer and burgers at one of the taverns. The tone of the area is upscale, but pleasantly so; if there is a certain clubbishness, visitors are never excluded. Madison Park Hardware, just north of Madison on 42nd Avenue East, may have more items for sale per square foot than any store in the city.

Walk back toward downtown on Madison, up the hill to 36th Avenue. Pause at 38th. On your right, at 3726 East Madison, is the Samuel Hyde house, a huge imposing mansion that would seem even more so except that it is sited at an angle to the street and is surrounded by trees; thus many pass by it without notice. Pause again at 37th, where on your left across Madison is a giant catalpa street tree, a beauty with very large leaves. In the sidewalk as you climb the hill are tiles to indicate street names, one of only a handful of such places where you'll find this in Seattle.

At 36th, turn left. The climbing is not over, but this is much pleasanter. The houses are nice (1117 an especially handsome stucco), though the level of pretension rises as you near the top of the hill, and gets quite out of control in two monsters, a recent one on the southeast corner of East Ward, and an older one, 808—the home of the president of the University of Washington. But the houses barely matter here, because the street is dominated by large wonderful American and English elms lining both sides. One long block over, on 34th, is a good row of katsuras on the east side, and east of 37th on East Prospect is another of plane trees. In the yards, in addition to the usual firs, cedars, and maples, are many green ashes. The effect is of age and settledness, a harmonizing of private and public space that diminishes the difference between resident and visitor. We will note a similar effect, achieved in two different ways, later on.

Turn left on Prospect, and go down the row of planes to 38th. In the alley on your right is a sign telling you not to drive in for 3802 or 3715 East Prospect. Walk into the alley, see a sign at 3802 about where deliveries should be made, and I can almost guarantee that you will feel you are eight years old and peeking at something forbidden. This may make the houses seem grander than they are, though 3802, known as the Baillargeon house, was once the home of Richard Fuller and his wife—he being the founder of the Seattle Art Museum and a man of exquisite taste. Too bad you cannot peek inside at the Mark Tobey mural, *Modal Tides,* but in late fall and winter you can glimpse the formal garden on the east side of the house.

Make your way back to 36th, turn left, and leave Washington Park by its steep southern slope, past a clutch of mostly stucco houses on your way down. Turn left on Lake Washington Boulevard, then a softish right onto Dorffel almost immediately; that's an Oriental plane in the triangle. On your right is a sight that is often repeated along this ridge, and is always fun: houses above

American and English elms making a cathedral on 36th Avenue East

houses, which makes the ones on top seem grand. More on this later. Around the bend are two brown shingle houses, 260 and 270 Dorffel Drive East, designed by Ellsworth Storey early in the century and immortalized in Victor Steinbrueck's *Seattle Cityscape*. They are especially nicely placed in relation to each other.

The next cross street is East John, and you should duck down onto it, to 3802, on your left, which is nestled at the foot of some steps amid a grove of rhododendrons. For years this was the home of one of the Northwest's premier poets, Theodore Roethke. On the evidence of the poems, Roethke spent few happy times indoors anywhere:

> How terrible the need for solitude:
> That appetite for life so ravenous
> A man's a beast prowling in his own house,
> A beast with fangs, and out for his own blood
> Until he finds the thing he almost was
> When the pure fury first raged in his head
> And trees came closer with a denser shade.
>   "The Pure Fury"

It was not, clearly, a house in which nothing happened. And looking down from the street, you can imagine being inside and have the trees come closer.

If trees are in leaf, turn around and go right on Maiden Lane down to the end, to 300, an intimate view of a grand house, designed by Arthur Loveless in the 1920s, with a feel for brick and traditional English house design matched in Seattle only by Fred Anhalt. If trees are bare, the house is best seen looking up from near the corner of 39th, Lake Washington Boulevard, and McGilvra down below, further on in this walk.

Come back up onto Dorffel, turn right on upper Maiden Lane

when the road splits, to the lily pond and perhaps the city's most attractive bus shelter, called Denny Blaine Lake Park. Across the street is Ellsworth Storey's chapel for Epiphany Church; it is on the left, the main church on the right. It is usually locked, but whenever the church office—behind the chapel and designed by Storey in the same style—is open, someone will be glad to let you in for a look. There are so few good looking and good feeling churches in Seattle, you should not miss this one. Outside and in, what is remarkable is how sculpted and decorated everything looks without ever giving the sense of being busy, cluttered, or rococo.

Now go behind the church property to East Howell, then turn south on 37th Avenue. Soon, on your right—harder to see when the leaves are out but still definitely there—is one of the ridge's best examples of a house above houses, the one on top known officially as the Charles Russell house but locally as The Castle. It is an ocher stucco with a Victorian turret, impressive rather than handsome, most impressive from down below.

At the corner of 37th and East Pine, a sidewalk leads downhill. Wind with it, keep winding, getting a nice feeling (contrast it to the one in the alley back on East Prospect) of legally walking through other peoples' yards—a different way to meld public and private. The sidewalk leads to Madrona Drive, where, across the street and to your left, you'll see a fine pair of almost matching houses and, on your right, a row of 1980s houses that rank with the worst new houses in Seattle—bare, brutal, arrogant, pointless every one. In a time when domestic architecture enjoyed such a revival, these are inexcusable; fifty years of growing trees and shrubs will only hide the shame.

Worse, to give these houses views from their back sides, many trees were cut down, so that what had been the totally magical effect of being on the East Pine Street bridge is less than it once

Ellsworth Storey's Epiphany Chapel

was. You are supposed to be surrounded by trees here, and now only half of you is. Still, it is one of the city's finest footbridges, wooden, T-shaped; and the house on the left, 3900 East Pine, is the only house in the city, maybe the country, that can be arrived at only by bridge.

Keep straight on Pine and you will come out, with a nice feeling of having emerged, to face a good stucco house on the corner of Pine and 40th. Left then on 40th, and the last house on the right is a lovely small Ellsworth Storey brown shingle house. Just as the road turns to go up to Evergreen Place, drop down the steps on the right onto Lake Washington Boulevard. Turn left, and soon, on your right, is 128, the Canadian Consulate with its sign in English and French. This is the beginning of what may be the finest grouping of grand houses in Seattle. It is not known as such, for two reasons, which only seem odd. First, grand houses are, in most people's minds, hard to get to, like the Fuller house you snuck up on earlier, and like those in The Highlands or in Hilltop (outside the city limits and the scope of this book). These, on the great Olmsted arterial, built when ordinary folk lived near streetcar lines far from here, are now on a heavily trafficked road. Thus people who can approach something easily can get easy with it. Second, most of these houses are not accessible to being looked at from the street, so this is a stretch that works best when leaves are off trees. Even then it requires slow walking to see how fine these houses are, and few people walk slowly here.

As the Boulevard starts to go up at an angle of 10 o'clock, take the turn to the right, into Denny Blaine Park, which has some fine lindens and birches and Seattle's largest Japanese cedars. It also has a nice beach—no raft, no lifeguard, no amenities, a kind of private public space that contrasts nicely with the very private homes nearby, whose residents never use the beach and have their own pools.

Back up Lake Washington Boulevard now, take the first right, on McGilvra, an apparently ordinary good street that is worth careful attention. First, it is a prime example of the Olmsted principle: build where streetcars don't run. Thus, near Lake Washington Boulevard are old houses, far from the streetcar line on Madison, and far grander than the bungalows equally old you will see as McGilvra reaches Madison a little less than a mile down the way. Then, especially in the first stretch, before the road splits, come perhaps Lake Washington ridge's finest examples of houses on top of houses, sometimes three tiers of them here, making a "scene" that neutralizes local defects or horrors in individual houses. Finally, though the feel of McGilvra is of an older street, in fact the houses here are of every decade of the century, which means a jumble of styles, prices, and pretensions. The effect is far from jumbly, though, largely because of the even setbacks from the street. The topography is generally level on the east side, hilly on the west. This yields, on the east, flat lawns and recessed grand houses at the outset, followed by houses close to the sidewalk after the road is one again, and, on the west, an astonishing achievement of harmony, despite a sometimes bizarre enjambment of house styles. A surprising street.

Your walk ends on Madison, where your car is or where a #11 bus will soon be. What I enjoy most about this walk is the way some of the nicest things are tucked away as befits a wooded ridge. But then, even better, some are tucked away in plain sight.

Walk 2: the longest in this book. Three hours or more (I offer suggestions for those who want to walk and drive).
Bus: #14 to the corner of Mount Rainier Drive and South Ferris.

The strong, steady hands of the Olmsteds can be felt throughout this walk, but maybe what is most interesting here is what hap-

Houses above houses on McGilvra Boulevard

pens when, if the Olmsteds were the cat, they went away and the mice got to playing.

From the bus stop, walk east a little on Ferris to Cascadia. This is one of Seattle's better best streets, like Federal, or West Highland: expensive, attractive, mostly unoriginal. Cascadia to your right as you hit it here is nice, but it gets its best marks to the left and north. The Olmsteds did their only laying out of house lots here, and the way it shows is similar to what happened on McGilvra: equal setbacks of houses of different styles and building materials creating a harmony, though here the fact that most of the houses are of the same time, about 1905–15, will lend its own harmony. Note, thus, how unpleasant 2820 and 2810 Cascadia seem here, precisely because they break this setback code. Before you get to these two, though, you will have noticed a grand stucco house, 3036 Cascadia, which you can keep in your mind as the other very nice houses begin to blur, until you reach the pièce de résistance, where Cascadia runs into Mount Baker Drive, and there is a spectacular view of the lake and the Cascades to the north. Here the neighborhood derives its name, and 2601 on the left, a superb stucco, just may be the best in the city.

(If you have driven here, park near South Ferris, walk up and back on Cascadia, then drive the walk until you get to 35th Avenue in Madrona.)

Go down Mount Baker Drive, cross McClellan, and turn a quick left onto Mount Baker Boulevard. This is the southernmost Olmsted reach, a lovely turning road with grand trees in its median, winding down to Franklin High School. The houses here have little of the ambition of those on Cascadia, as is consistently the case on the ridge's western slope, but the boulevard itself is as good as one gets. I am convinced that the general opinion, that Franklin High, the design of Edgar Blair in 1912, may be the best looking of Seattle's older high schools, derives about equally from the street, the building's handsome west façade, and Fred Bassetti's superb restoration in the late 1980s.

You are now going to climb up the side of the ridge, and observe the first of three stretches, none of which was planned as Cascadia and Mount Baker Boulevard were planned, each of which extends to you a somewhat different message. First turn north on 31st, the arterial here, uphill, for a mile or more. This is a fine ordinary street, but since most of Seattle's older neighborhoods have such a street, it is best contemplated just because it is characteristic. These are contractor houses, built in the teens and twenties mostly—small lots, gables and eaves, the dead middle of the middle class. These are good houses for childless couples and the retired, but they really need kids, and to get kids they need good surrounding public schools, of a kind Seattle has had too little of for too long. It was precisely these people who left Seattle when mandatory busing was instituted in 1977 and the schools were not good enough to hold them. In this particular case there are enough middle-class blacks to keep the houses up and the street stable, but this is a good place to check for For Sale signs to gauge how well it, and the city, are doing.

At the top of the hill, turn right on South Day and contemplate, first the large house on the southwest corner of 32nd, then its neighbors. It is a Victorian beauty, built before Cascadia, probably before Lake Washington Boulevard. Now go back to 31st and get onto 30th Avenue via Norman and Yakima to see something similar. This area was once called Rainier Heights, and in one of their original plans the Olmsteds had Lake Washington Boulevard climbing the entire slope to get here. Why? Because of some grand houses on 30th, most notably the Judge Ronald house, a large white colonial on the west side that is on the National Register of Historic Places. Also because people were just beginning to want to build houses with views that faced water and mountains rather than downtown, and from the corner of 31st and King on a clear day you could see Mount St. Helens before it erupted. But also to keep out the Employed. In his report to the park board, J. C. Olmsted wrote: "Undoubtedly it would be a wise policy for the city to acquire the whole of this hillside. There is every probability that if this is not done it will be occupied by cheap houses, the existence of which in the proximity to one of the best residential districts in the city would tend to retard the rise in value of that district which its natural advantages should otherwise ensure." The city did acquire a good deal of the hillside, and Lake Washington Boulevard as built did leave the lakeshore at Leschi, wind its way through Frink and Colman parks, then come back to the lake at Mount Baker Park. Perhaps because the Boulevard did not climb all the way to Rainier Heights, the land here on 30th was not developed in parcels, and "one of the best residential districts in the city" never quite came about. The Olmsteds proposed, time disposed.

As you continue on 30th north of Yesler, you may be aware of a change without quite knowing what it is. This is upper Leschi, which was named a Model Cities neighborhood in the late 1960s. Model Cities was one of Lyndon Johnson's Great Society projects, and upper Leschi was a perfect choice because at the time its housing stock was both excellent and badly run down. The federal money mostly went for undergrounding the power lines, and if you cannot make a silk purse out of a sow's ear, if you start trying at a time when other expansionary energies are loose, you can come close. In the last twenty years new houses have gone up, almost all of which were designed to blend with their neighbors. There was plenty of rehabilitation too—new top floors, cantilevering, new upper-story dormers. On 30th and nearby streets you have something old that also looks spanking new, another of Seattle's great recycling achievements in the last generation.

Turn right on either James or Cherry, cross the invisible boundary between Leschi and Madrona, and make your way to 35th. Turn right again and go down to the end of the street, to another viewpoint from which you could once see Mount St. Helens. What singles this out from other viewpoints along the ridge are the three houses on the headland to your right. They were designed by Wendell Lovett in the early 1980s. When the first one went up, it seemed just another contemporary rectangular brute, but the three together play a theme and variations game—best seen from here rather than close up—that architects usually leave it to contractors to play.

Now walk north on 35th. If you have driven and parked here, you will need to walk down and back. This street, never known as one of Seattle's better bests, is worth careful attention, especially in contrast to Cascadia in Mount Baker and Rainier Heights. An early streetcar line came out East Union, turned on 34th and swung down and around to the lake. Soon after, another came out East Cherry to 34th. One block from the streetcar, 35th, a flat street along the ridge, offered fine views for house builders as early as the 1890s. Some of the notable very early houses are the Raymond/Ogden mansion at 702 35th, the unnumbered house (recently redone) on the northwest corner of Spring, the small Victorian at 1115, 1415 on a huge double lot with a couple of outstanding madrona trees, and 1525. These all were built before the idea of keeping "cheap houses" away from "best residential districts," and so the simple folk built here too. There are houses from every era in the past century, newer elegance as well as older—houses that would better fit elsewhere, St. Therese's church and schoolyard, an odd stucco house on the southeast corner of Marion that someone is forever restoring without finishing the job.

The great house on 35th is 712, rightly and wrongly known as the Mary McCarthy house. In *Memories of a Catholic Girlhood,* McCarthy writes that she spent her early years in a "brick house on Twenty-fourth Avenue." City directories of the time, plus the photographs in her book, show the house was actually 934 22nd North (now designated East), just north of Holy Names Academy. After the death of her parents in the 1918 flu epidemic, she endured five years with her father's relatives in Minneapolis. She was rescued by her maternal grandfather, Harold Preston, senior partner in what is now Preston Thorgrimson Shidler Gates & Ellis, always one of Seattle's most prestigious law firms. He lived at 712 35th, and though this was McCarthy's official home until she went to college, she spent most of her adolescence at area boarding schools. As life became interesting elsewhere, 712 35th's many hours of silence became dreary for McCarthy, but earlier it was "an enchanted house, which was full of bulges" with "two overhanging balconies, on the lake side, and four bays and a little tower . . . : the bay-window seat in the parlor, the cabinet with opaline Tiffany glass and little demitasse cups, all different, the grass wallpaper, the pongee-silk curtains, the sleeping porches upstairs, the hawthorn tree in front." From the street you can see or easily imagine all this. The area above the front porch has as its only feature a small circular window, which makes it look like a porthole on a ship, an oddly pleasing effect. The current owners have painted it a goodly full teal, and their busy landscaping in front seems quite appropriate. All in all, one of the most interesting houses in Seattle. McCarthy's descriptions of it come in the last chapter of *Memories,* the one devoted to her grandmother, the one most about Seattle.

You are now at the northern reach of your walk. If you want

712 35th Avenue, the "Mary McCarthy house," one of the most interesting in the city

to take a break, over in the small shopping area centered at 34th and Union you can find coffee and something to eat most daytime hours at the Hi-Spot Cafe or Cool Hand Luke's. Afterwards, you can do it a number of ways. (Driving, follow the route of the #2 bus down to Lake Washington Boulevard. Take the boulevard south, stay on it as it leaves the lake and climbs up over the I-90 tunnel, take a right at Mount Baker Park, then your first left, Shoreland Drive, which will lead you out near where you began.) You can hop on a #2 going down to the lake, get a transfer, walk a mile or so south, hop on a #27 also going south, to where it leaves the lake, walk down to Mount Baker Park, turn right, then left up Shoreland, and you can swing up it, past Cascadia, and catch the #14 with time still left on your transfer. Or, having lots of energy left, you can wind your way down through Madrona by any number of routes—there are lots of public steps through here—end up at Lake Washington Boulevard about where it leaves the lake, wind up, down, and around with it to Mount Baker Park, and so up Shoreland to Cascadia, to your car or bus.

As to what you might see along the way: some excellent houses on top of houses, as always best seen when trees are bare; some good bends in roads, and, once on Lake Washington Boulevard when it leaves the lake, two outstanding places and facts. First, notice 100 Lake Washington Boulevard South, which looks perfectly ordinary as you approach it from the northeast, but which tapers shockingly to a point on its southwest end. This is next to an amazing structure that looks like a bridge except nothing can pass over it, and that is all that is left of the old Leschi streetcar line. Then, as you wind out of Frink Park about half a mile further along the boulevard, you come to a stretch with some of the best views on the ridge. Since the Olmsteds assumed that Lake Washington Boulevard would always be honey for very well-fed bears, they must have thought this would become "one of the city's best residential districts." Not a bit of it. These are just about the most ordinary houses on the entire ridge, and more power to them.

Finally, Shoreland Drive—for one last go at how a street came to be as it is. Many houses on Shoreland were built in the Olmsted era, many were not, and some date from after World War II. But the result is never like 35th in Madrona because the steep slope down to the lake demands that houses be much closer to the street than is normal in Seattle. And because nothing can be built on the even steeper slope above, the houses can be jammed together and still enjoy excellent privacy. It is the ultimate in setback harmonizing, and I do not know another street quite like it in the city.

14 Seward Park

When the city of Seattle acquired Bailey Peninsula and called it Seward Park—Seward was President Andrew Johnson's secretary of state, and he was responsible for the purchase of Alaska in 1867, and Alaska was a major theme in the Exposition of 1909—there was no Seattle to speak of south of the Mount Baker district and east of Rainier Valley. Lake Washington Boulevard was laid out down to Seward Park, but the road was not paved beyond Mount Baker for a long time. Most houses in the Seward Park neighborhood date from after World War II and suffer from what a friend of mine, who herself lives in just such a house, once called "a bad case of the 50s." There are some excellent things in the neighborhood, mostly the result either of Arthur Loveless designing an enclave of houses between Seward Park Drive and the lake, or else of its being the closest thing Seattle has to a Jewish neighborhood, which means temples that generally look better than most of Seattle's Christian churches, a couple of kosher groceries, and men and boys in yarmulkes, all helping to try to make more interesting what otherwise is enervatingly the same. But the real interest for a visitor is the park, and it is one of Seattle's very best.

Walk: a circuit along the water takes about forty-five minutes, and a hike in the wilderness another forty-five minutes; the two can be shortened and combined for a walk of a little over an hour.

Bus: #39 to South Juneau, a block west of the park.

At the entrance to the park, stop and be one of few to read the signs on the monument. It celebrates a "growing friendship" between Japan and the United States by having Japanese cherries planted around it. The date is 1929. Another plaque, put up in 1930, expresses thanks for help given by people in Seattle after Japan's 1923 earthquake. A year later the Japanese invaded Manchuria, eleven years later came the attack on Pearl Harbor, sixteen years later atomic bombs were dropped on Hiroshima and Nagasaki. After that, we had survivals of arrogance, ignorance, and competitiveness on both sides. If not a "growing friendship," then, it's something that oddly might include that, as the fates of the two countries keep becoming more entwined. A similar marker, and planting, the lettering in Japanese, is a hundred yards or so north on Lake Washington Boulevard, and this time the cherries are much more in evidence.

From the entrance, you go right, counterclockwise, for reasons that become clear later. On the south side, along the water, is a splendid view of Mount Rainier and south Lake Washington, and, on the land side, above the many signs that say POISON OAK (rare but truly native in western Washington), is the largest stand of madrona trees in the city. Others, like the grove on the west edge of the University of Washington campus, or on Magnolia Bluff, may stand out more because their surroundings are barer, but this one continues for a quarter mile or more, and intermittently around the peninsula after that.

The splendor of madronas can be felt by people any age, but for those who have fewer years left than they have had, madronas are unique. Madronas in cities are in chronically poor health, subject to this or that disease, yet they take a wonderfully long time to die. My favorite tree in Seattle is the lone madrona a couple of miles up Lake Washington Boulevard from here; it has been dying since I first noticed it twenty-odd years ago, but it is still not dead.

The east side of the peninsula is the best, and best seen around sunrise or on any afternoon warm enough that the shade is welcome. For most of the mile there are deciduous trees between the path and the water to contrast with the conifers and other evergreens on the inner slopes. The feeling is of a tunnel that does not enclose, but almost. At the far end, the pavement goes straight ahead, the deciduous trees fall away, the view opens out, and you can walk or run a couple of hundred yards as if you were about to go off the edge, all the time knowing you will turn left at the last minute. Adventure, safe adventure, a signature for Seattle.

The path is pastoral, the setting is wilderness. Mercer Island as you go up the east side seems sparsely populated, so the view of downtown's tallest buildings after you turn west can be jarring, like some looming adults come to break up the children's games. You may, in response, want to find and take the path that leads straight up into the forest. If so, if you stick to this trail and keep heading south, in twenty minutes or so you will come out onto the paved road that bisects the peninsula. From there, take a right and you will find yourself coming out at the art studio, with the park entrance at a ten o'clock angle. Let us say, though, that you want to continue the water walk, and do wilderness later.

There may be problems as you start down the west side: raw, prevailing southwest wind in winter, hot sun on warm after-

Seward Park, safe adventure on its northeast corner

noons, masses of large pleasure boats anchored such that a friend of mine calls this Thorstein Veblen Bay. Whatever mood these put you in, when you pick up another line of trees between you and the water, the path jogs left, you're out of the wind or sun, and soon you come out of trees into light as you did as the northeast end, but with a quite different feeling: arrival, finish. Welcome things such as water and toilets are just down the way on the left.

Except in the middle of the day, there are always enough people on the path to let one feel safe. But it is not people one wants here but trees, light and shade, reflections on water, and a distinctive, unurban sense that though seasons and weather bring changes, Seward Park is always essentially the same —wilderness pastoral.

To get a full sense of "wilderness" here, you need to go into the forest. The easiest way to do this is to walk up the paved road that starts just south of the art studio—past the picnic areas— to the top, where you have an amphitheater on your right and a trail leading into the forest on your left. Much of this was never logged and except for the one in O. O. Denny Park (in Juanita east of the lake) this is the largest old-growth forest in the area. There are trees here that were mature when white settlers first came to Alki Point, and it feels like it.

Since what you want to do is to get lost, or at least feel lost, I need describe no route. You have only slightly less than a square mile here, and in addition to the well-worn 8 to 10 foot wide paths, you will find numerous lesser paths hinting of real lostness tempting you. Some are false and stop at a fallen log or a stump, some wind and fork and eventually come out onto some other trail. On the main trails you may occasionally encounter another person; on the side trails, never. The only sounds are those made by you or birds.

As for the trees, since this is native forest, you will find nothing unfamiliar; almost everything will be fir, cedar, hemlock, madrona, cherry, dogwood maple, yew, or oak. It is size and age that one can revel in, or be amazed at. Douglas firs of more than 20 feet around are not uncommon here, and when you come on a fallen beauty you can start with "George Bush elected" on the outside and count your way back to "Theodore Roosevelt elected" quite easily, and back to "Abraham Lincoln elected" often. You can also pass "Remember Pearl Harbor," "Remember the Maine," and "Remember the Alamo," though I doubt you will be able to get back to Bunker Hill or Saratoga. However you do it, you are bound to feel, looking at the tree, that it is more impressive than human history. Hold on to that feeling for as long as you can.

For birds the best I can tell you is that a bald eagle is usually in residence, and I always hear some calls or songs that I never hear at home. Bring binoculars and find out.

To write about the Seward Park wilderness would seem to be to advertise it—to guarantee that the next time you go, you will not be alone. Perhaps, but I doubt it. The reason Bailey Peninsula was old-growth forest in 1911 is that it was at the edge of the city, beyond the consciousness of most Seattleites. It still is. The water walk is beloved of thousands, most of whom live in the south end. For most who live north of Lake Union, enough people to make up a U.S. congressional district, Seward Park is a name only, the end of a bike trip maybe, and no one bikes the wilderness trails. So the thrill of getting off a city bus and being able, within twenty minutes, to wander solitary in a wilderness awaits you. Schmitz Park in West Seattle is also wilderness and little used, but its total area is much smaller.

15 West Seattle

P eople who live, say, in Wallingford or Madison Park, who may think nothing of driving to Bellevue to shop, to Stevens Pass to ski, or to the Skagit Valley to see the tulips, usually can think of no reason to go to West Seattle, except maybe to get a ferry to Vashon Island. Seattle's most exciting bridge is the new West Seattle span over the Duwamish, one of Seattle's most engaging water walks is from Alki Point to Duwamish Head, two of Seattle's finest parks are Lincoln and Schmitz, yet the people you see in these places are mostly West Seattle locals. It is like another country.

LINCOLN PARK

Bus: #54 from Second and Union.

Lincoln is less than half the size of Seward Park, a quarter the size of Discovery, but for variety of uses it is Seattle's best park: softball fields, a football field, tennis courts, horseshoe pits, playground equipment, a long beach, plenty of barbecue pits and picnic tables, a heated saltwater swimming pool.

Given all this, there is nothing like wilderness at Lincoln, but it is very easy to get off by yourself (ves). From the #54 bus stop at the south end (there is a parking lot a little further to the south) bear northwest, keep the snack bar and horseshoe pits on your right, bear left when the path splits, right at the next opportunity, and soon you will be at the bluff, with a path cutting along its edge at right angles to you, another winding down the ridge to the beach. Take the ridge path to your left, and soon there is a fine viewpoint to the west; then you are surrounded by a stand of madronas as the path moves down to the beach.

At the bottom, go right along the paved path next to the beach. Along the stony part of the beach you can explore some of the best tidepools on Seattle's coastline, and on the sandy part you can dig for clams or watch others clam. Especially if it is cloudy, cool, or rainy, you can have the walk to yourself. And with nothing but water, forest, and mountains to the west and north, you can imagine that you recently disembarked from the *Exact,* the steamer that brought the first white settlers to Alki Point in November 1851.

The pavement stops a short way from the north end of the park. If you go back the way you came, you will not imagine you are among the first white settlers, but the views down the Sound are fine. Or you can climb the bluff and walk back south by any route you choose.

Lincoln Park demands no response from its visitor, and you need try to sustain no particular mood. Go with someone else, or with a bunch. It's all quite open, sociable when need be, quite different from the park to the north that's up next.

SCHMITZ PARK

Bus: #56 from First Avenue to Admiral Way and S. W. Stevens.

The only Schmitz Park amenities, if they can be so called, are a

Fallen trees in the Schmitz Park wilderness

parking lot and some trails. The rest is virgin forest. It is much smaller than the Seward Park wilderness, but, for as long as it lasts, equally impressive, and, in respect to fallen trees, even more so. Along the left-hand trail, not far from the parking lot, are two uprooted firs, probably not more than 100 feet in height, but with an exposed root system that may be the largest you or I will ever see. It's so quiet here it can feel eerie; in other parks you may feel lucky to be alone, while here you might feel lucky if one or two others are nearby.

CALIFORNIA AVENUE S.W.

Bus: #22 from First Avenue. Or #37 (by way of Alki and Beach Drive S.W.) from Second and Pike.

The way it was. Though California Avenue is the longest straight road in Seattle, it is mainly the two long blocks between Oregon and Edmunds that we are interested in here. It is known to locals as The Junction, though Junction Feed and Seed is the only sign remaining of its original status. There are 75,000 residents of West Seattle, and many do not shop here; nor is California as able as North 45th in Wallingford or even East Madison to provide all a local on foot could want. What is remarkable is a sense that you are in a time warp, on a street of the late 1940s or 1950s. This is not a strip or a run, but Main Street. The scale is small, the conversation neighborly, the traffic of little bother. Nearby Michael J. Fox found his parents, and Peggy Sue got married. The Mediterranean Gothic Holy Rosary Church is a block east of California (4139 42nd S.W.) and the California and Alaska St. Brewery is a brewpub, and just a few doors south of where it says it is. Both are worth a look or a stop.

If you are driving, at the north end of California, as it starts down-

California Avenue S.W., leftover from the 1950s

hill toward the Sound, is Hamilton Viewpoint, one of the city's finest—something close to a 270 degree view stretching from Magnolia Bluff around to the container cargo cranes of the Port of Seattle to the south. It is a fine place from which to pick out and name the downtown buildings you know, because it is up high and facing downtown straight on. But the special feature of Hamilton is the view at night. You are too far away to get anything like the Emperor View of downtown, but you get Queen Anne, Interbay, Magnolia, and Ballard stretching out to the north—all lights making these areas look more involved in city life than they ever do during the day.

ALKI TO DUWAMISH HEAD

Walk: thirty to forty minutes each way.
Bus: #37 to 63rd S.W. near Alki Point, from Second Avenue.

It is a good walk here either way; if you are arriving by bus, you must start from the western end, and if you are driving, it is best done parking at Duwamish Head. I will describe these walks as though they were totally different, but you will quickly see they are not.

Walking west from Duwamish, you find that the road makes a saucerlike semicircle along the water and the path is lanes alongside the road. The weathers of choice here are opposite to each other: in high summer, on a California-come-north cloudless day, go when boats are out and the Olympics are on display; in the rainy season, the best time is when a low pressure front is coming at you fresh from the Sound, and the air is pure Alaska. In many of Seattle's freshwater areas the Canada geese have driven away other water birds. Here you seldom see a goose, and loons, cormorants, and buffleheads appear along with mallards, coots, and gulls. A sea mammal comes up for air, harbor seals mostly, but whales are not unknown.

On most of Seattle's water walks, especially on Green Lake and Seward Park, people around you are Getting Exercise. This is different; the ratio of cyclers and joggers to the whole is small. West Seattle families come down to look at the view, or teenagers come to do what teenagers do with each other. After about a mile, the path comes into its own as a beach walk, and you are "away," at some seaside resort. Driftwood fires are allowed here, you need be in no hurry, you can stop to get warm, or heat the hot dog you remembered to bring. Alki has a reputation for difficulty between the young and the police, but that is almost entirely a matter of ten warm-weather weekends.

When you reach 63rd S.W., the beach abruptly halts, and you will see a plaque. It gives the names of the original people who landed off the *Exact,* but is an even greater failure than most historic plaques, since it offers only names and commemoration of an irrelevant event. (What is needed here is the kind of thing you can find a mile to the south, at Beach Drive S.W. and S.W. Carroll, at the Weather Watch Park.) Since you don't have a copy of *Seattle Past to Present* to hand, the short course reads: the first white settlers spent the winter of 1851–52 here, then moved, to avoid the nasty prevailing southwest winds, across Elliott Bay to what is now downtown Seattle. They had come to seek their fortune. Some found it, some found and lost it, some discovered they were interested in something else. All worked hard, and there is little existing record of serious strife among these people. After they abandoned the site, West Seattle became accessible only by ferry, and soon was the foreign territory it seems to have remained to the present.

As you turn and walk back to the east, you will be able to feel more strongly than on the outward journey that you are at a resort. Alongside the road, of the thirty or more businesses, only the Taco Bell is a franchise. The others are a combination of caterers to visitors, mostly places to eat, and local establishments like the Alki Market. Stop and eat at Spud's, for fish and chips. Alki Avenue seems more of a promenade going this way. Then, when the path leaves the beach, it is apartments and bungalows across the way. All is still in the same spirit of "away," though. The apartments are cousins to motels in Grants Pass, Oregon, and the bungalows, originally summer homes, are nicely weathered and funky. If you have seen Riviera Place N.E. in Lake City or Perkins Lane in Magnolia replace their old summer homes with mini-mansions, you will especially like this. Keep an eye out for the sign that proudly says "Boeing Company Management Parking Only."

As you reach Duwamish Head, the resort disappears, and the view of downtown gets better and better as you turn the corner. It ends up being a rival for the one above at Hamilton, and for the ones at Gas Works Park or Kerry Park.

When Charles Royer became mayor in 1978, he took with him, or so it was alleged, a copy of *Seattle Past to Present,* in which you can find it said, about the skyscraper boom of the early 1970s, "The end of this spate of building is probably now in sight, and its results are far from being all good." As prognosticator I was lousy of course, since the boom had ten years to run, and Royer, who loved it all, said when he left office in 1990, "Seattle feels more like a big city now." Anyone who is doubtful if having all those buildings was a good thing can reply that Seattle now feels like other cities its size that had skyscraper booms in the 1970s and 1980s, like Columbus and Sacramento.

Seen from Duwamish Head, though, it is hard to think that way about downtown. The most architecturally boring buildings, the ones most killing to street-level life, here are part of a great sky-line. Nothing is framed, as it is at Gas Works. The very

Alki Avenue S.W., among the few surviving beach houses from an earlier time

massiveness of some of the buildings, since you are seeing them all from below, makes them seem to soar. You are of the scene, but not in it. Before the boom, the tallest structures in this skyline were the Space Needle and the Smith Tower, and, looking at the scene from here, it is hard to want that time back again.

From Second and Yesler, from Second and Madison, from Kerry Park, from Gas Works, and now from Duwamish, it seems important to keep trying to understand the recent history of Seattle's downtown from different angles. It never looks better than from here, and it does make Seattle feel more like a big city too.

16 Magnolia Bluff and Discovery Park

Magnolia is mostly miles and miles of upper bourgeois tedium, streets with horrible names like Viewmont, Parkmont, Eastmont, and Westmont, most houses dating from the 1920s to the 1960s, uphill and downhill, all wires under-grounded, unbrokenly residential except for one shopping area around 32nd West and West McGraw. There is plenty of money in Magnolia, but the houses are ordinary, the landscaping and gardening are ordinary, and it is poor in trees. No one walks in Magnolia, I suspect because everywhere you go, *Plus ça change, plus c'est la même chose.* But there is one fine drive, and, at its end, one fine walk.

Walk: in Discovery Park, one hour to do the loop trail, plus time on the beach and in Daybreak Star Indian Cultural Center.
Bus: #33, from Fourth Avenue to the east entrance of Discovery Park. #24 goes through Central Magnolia but not into the park.

Driving, you leave downtown on Alaskan Way and Elliott Avenue. From the right lane, you take the Pier 91 and Magnolia Bridge turnoff, which loops around and then heads west over West Gar-

Madrona trees on Magnolia Boulevard

field Street. There was a famous labor skirmish near this bridge in the 1930s, and underneath it today is a winery. Once over the bridge, the arterial becomes West Galer, and then, when Thorndyke comes in from the north, it becomes Magnolia Boulevard. After half a mile the boulevard turns left, crosses the West Howe Street bridge, then swings left again and climbs to Magnolia Bluff. On your right is only ample evidence of the neighborhood's obsession with expensive ordinariness, but on the left is plenty of reason for you to take this stretch as slowly as the cars behind you allow. The area was named for the trees along the bluff, but the namer could not tell a magnolia from a madrona, and these madronas are stately creatures—throwbacks to a time before white folks, when so much of the Pacific coast was lined with them. Beyond the trees are marvelous views of the entire sweep of central Puget Sound, islands, and the Olympics. No need to stop to gaze here, though, as the Discovery Park walk offers much of the same.

The Boulevard stops at West Emerson. Turn right onto Emerson, and at 34th turn left, heading north until you reach Government Way, which leads to the left to Discovery Park's east entrance, where you park and go into the Visitor Center and get a map. Like so many of Seattle's parks, Discovery was created in the 1970s, when it was realized that one needed land to make a park, but not necessarily wilderness or total seclusion. This one was the result of long negotiations with the U.S. Army, which had dozily occupied a post on the site since the end of the nineteenth century. When push came to shove, and return of the land to the city was inevitable, the Army managed to keep a hunk of the central property. Simultaneously, groups of Indians stormed the post and demanded return of the entire property, holding out for a piece on the northwest border, where Daybreak Star Indian Cultural Center was built. Seattle's golfers also insisted they needed land for another municipal course, and they got as far as a vote before they were rejected. So it is Discovery Park, cum Daybreak Star, cum the Metro sewage station at West Point, cum the U.S. Army. In *Enjoying Seattle's Parks,* Brandt Morgan writes: "Discovery Park has the potential to become the greatest urban nature park in the nation." Given all its competing uses, this seems farfetched, but as long as you know what to expect, you can enjoy yourself here.

Get your bearings from the map, and set off on the loop trail to the north. After maybe five minutes the trail to Daybreak Star splits off; take it, down through the north parking lot, down again on a paved road for maybe ten more minutes. Along the way you will find an ample supply of blackberry bushes, full of fruit in midsummer, and the road ends at Daybreak Star.

Outside it isn't much, except for a stunning view to the northwest, up Sound toward Carkeek Park, with Shilshole Bay Marina and Golden Gardens Park in the foreground. Inside, huge cedar logs and beams set off two floors. The lower one is reserved for events. I once heard a steel drum concert here and the building took the sound joyously. The upper floor is dominated by seven paintings commissioned for the opening of Daybreak Star in 1977. Try to put Nathan Jackson's *Man and Killer Whale,* Robert Montoya's *Deer Hunter,* and Glen LaFontaine's *Buffalo Hunter* into your head, first individually, then collectively. Each is different in design and color, but each places hunter and hunted in sympathetic relation to each other, which is something Hemingway and others have tried to do, and failed. Since this hunting is seldom done any more, the paintings are shining testimony to the strength of traditions and tribal memory.

Outside again, past the parking lot is a paved trail. In about ten minutes it joins the loop trail, and you go right. If you want to go to the beach, take the paved road down to the Metro plant.

Straight ahead is probably the oldest structure in the city, the small Coast Guard lighthouse built in 1881 at West Point (its first lamps were lit by whale oil). Visiting hours are weekend afternoons. To your left is a sandy beach, to your right a rocky one, each about a mile in length. Intertidal life is best to the north, beachcombing and clamming best to the south. Of special interest are the fragile cliffs on the south side—layers of gray, gold, brown, the lowest dating back to times before the last Ice Age. The ranger at the Visitor Center can name the geological events of each layer.

Go back up the hill until you see married soldiers' housing on your right. Go right, and you're deep in woods. None of this is old growth, but the trees are as old as the century. Then you're out into meadow, with the 1900 army buildings in the distance to your left, views down Sound on your right. With all the human activity fairly near, it is surprising how good the bird watching is. Bald eagles are frequently seen here, sparrow hawks dive for rodents in the meadow. Recently I saw two flickers at work on adjacent trees, plus two large and strangely colored rabbits.

After the meadow there is a rise into another parking lot, then it is five minutes downhill back to the Visitor Center. Even if you've left the loop trail to go to the Indian Center and the beach, you probably will not have walked more than five miles, but because of the ups, downs, and shifts in landscape, it can feel like a lot more. Too typical of Magnolia, alas: if at the end you'd like anything more than a water fountain and a toilet, they are a few miles away.

Coast Guard lighthouse, Discovery Park

17 Woodland Park Zoo

Green Lake

Guy Phinney was the first person to show that Seattle's climate was perfect for an English garden and park. Where he created these was not Seattle when he bought 200 acres southwest of Green Lake to develop as an estate, this in 1887. He laid out roads, lawns, and flower beds near an impressive stone entrance at North 50th and Fremont. He built a gate house for his family, but died before the mansion could be done. The city of Seattle bought the land from his widow in 1899, extended the city limits north to include the new property, and eventually constructed a streetcar line to connect with the one Phinney had built up Fremont Avenue.

The Olmsteds were delighted with all Phinney had done, and left gardens, park, and forest mostly as they found them, adding roads, and doing some clearing to allow for the building of a small zoo. The zoo uses 1904 as its date of origin, since that is when it is first mentioned in the city's annual report, although from then on the city itself has seldom shown any interest in having a zoo, or supporting it. Most additions were made from private donations, and no admission was charged until the zoo got serious in the 1970s. Meanwhile, lower Woodland was developed to include picnic tables, tennis courts, soccer fields, a nine-hole pitch-putt golf course, and one of the city's two lawn bowling greens. Houses were built near Green Lake before the turn of the century, and an early mayor, Wilbur Wood, lived nearby. Perhaps because Woodland Park, the zoo, and Green Lake were always "breathing places for the Employed," the residential neighborhoods that eventually surrounded them were never more than modest.

Since the visitors to Woodland Park were a "they" who were quite different from the Olmsted-minded Parks Department, why not have an amusement park alongside the zoo, and why mind if the animal exhibits at the zoo were based on a model of a medieval prison, where inmates were being punished and were not meant to be comfortable? The cages were small and bare, the open areas for elephants and bears bleak. To be sure, this was not uncommon in American zoos, and Woodland Park was one of the first zoos to use glass instead of bars to restrain their larger cats. Still, it took the general resurgence of energy of the 1970s for anything significant to happen.

The first things to happen did not actually happen, either. George Bartholick was hired to draw up a design for the zoo, and he soon envisaged lidding Aurora Avenue (which had bisected upper and lower Woodland in the 1930s) and extending the zoo's boundaries eastward to give the animals more space to move in. The plan was voted down, as bond issues for a children's zoo had been five times before that. Forward Thrust included in its bond issues money for new primate buildings; they were never built either, but for different reasons.

David Hancocks joined the zoo's design team in 1975, and a year later he became the zoo's director. An Englishman trained as an architect in zoo design, Hancocks had learned from the animals at Whipsnade, London's open air zoo, that they did not avail

themselves of the space they were given, because, he then learned, animals in the wild do not move around much except to find food and water. No need to extend the zoo's boundaries. Take out the amusement park, start charging admission, get serious about finding ways to make the animals themselves more comfortable and the people aware that the animals, in Henry Beston's great words, "are not brethren, they are not underlings; they are other nations, caught with ourselves in the net of life and time, fellow prisoners of the splendor and travail of earth."

A reptile house was provided, then, and a nocturnal house for animals small enough so that habitats can be created for them in enclosed indoor spaces. What followed in 1979 was the first major new habitat, designed by Jones & Jones, for gorillas, along with two others that proved unsuccessful, for Asian primates; a year later came the African savanna, for zebras, giraffes, spring-boks, land birds, hippos, patas monkeys, and, across a path, lions; a year later still a bare rock formation for Himalayan snow leopards. Throughout, graphics, tests, questions, designed by Education Curator Helen Freeman, to draw spectators closer to full attention. All this was done by the time Hancocks left in 1984.

Of course the savanna is not a savanna, and trees and logs do not make a forest habitat for gorillas. It is all based on illusions, first to let the animals relax, then to urge the people to forget where they know they are. Heated rocks abound, since it is cooler in Seattle than it ever is near the equator. Sightlines are established and blocked. The animals are taken indoors at night, and are fed so the herbivores do not destroy the vegetation and the carnivores other animals.

The city remains uninterested, or unimpressed, or wishes that Woodland Park were like Gas Works, where once done is done.

African savannah, at the zoo

Elsewhere, signs of success abound. The animals are breeding. Admission prices have been steadily raised and attendance goes up too. New director David Towne has found private donors, and in 1988 a model Thai village with a small crew of working Asian elephants was opened, followed in 1992 by the zoo's largest building, a tropical rain forest. Plans have been drawn up for six more extensive habitats, and if they all come about, most of the major ecological zones of the earth will be represented at Woodland Park.

No need to design a walk, since you can get a map when you enter and design your own. Here is a list of things to look for and remember that might enhance your pleasure:

1. Remember Guy Phinney, and spend some time looking at the roses if they are in bloom in the garden to the right of the zoo's south entrance. Once inside, notice the trees, as pleasing as any plantings in Seattle, except for the Arboretum and the University of Washington campus. Notable: the black locusts in the savanna, enormous pin oak and English laurel in the Family Farm.

2. Some animals frequently are hidden, and in the wildlife habitats all are allowed to hide. Snow leopards are shy, hippos sleep underwater for hours at a time, the lions are at a distance. But the giraffes are too large to hide, and the gorillas seldom want to.

3. The Asian elephants are best seen when they are taking a bath. Ask a keeper when that is going to happen next.

4. Though the cats in the Feline House are enclosed, much has been done to make their space "natural." Conversely, though, the open habitats in the north part of the zoo, especially those for the marsupials, the llamas, the North American bison, are all badly underdeveloped and discouraging.

5. At the time of the Tropical Forest's opening, the flora was wonderful, but inexplicably the insects, birds, and animals are

separated out, so you get about half the sense of a single environment you should have.

6. Read the signs, paying special attention to any passage quoting Henry Beston.

7. Though the zoo may be a "good place to take the kids," having kids in your charge will probably distract you. Go, if you can, with a good friend you suspect or know is more patient and observant than you are.

GREEN LAKE

Bus: #16 to East Green Lake from Third and Pike.

Seattle does not have a single great water walk, like the seawall in Stanley Garden in Vancouver, B.C. It has a plethora; but many, like Seward and Lincoln parks, are at the city's extremities and tend to be walked primarily by those living nearby. If the paths on the north and south sides of Union Bay were longer and did not end abruptly, if the University of Washington had had the foresight to create a walk on its southern border, if the Corps of Engineers had actually built a trail between Fremont and the locks as it has long threatened to do, Green Lake might have a rival for the city's affections. As it stands, however, Green Lake is not just Seattle's most popular water walk, but the most heavily used recreational space. From an hour before sunrise to an hour after sunset, people are there, usually many people. One reason, then, for its popularity, is that it is a scene, like Broadway, or Pike Place Market.

There are others. It is a flat 2.7 miles around, almost every sedentary person's idea of Exercise. Ravenna Boulevard to the east, leading to Cowen and Ravenna parks and the Burke-Gilman Trail, make it good for those who want to go farther. Though water fauna here is not as rich and varied as on the Sound, geese have never driven out other water birds. The inlets and bends in the path on the north side are attractive. There are boats, but none with motors. Cyclists, and even skateboarders, have never been forbidden, but they are not encouraged either, and the critical mass of people on foot often makes it uncomfortable for them. On the southeast, east, and north sides are a variety of places to eat and drink only a hundred yards away. The wind is often a factor, and does interesting things to the lake. The Bathhouse Theatre is a prime candidate for best small theatrical group in Seattle, and does wonders with tiny performing and seating spaces. Though I would never go to Green Lake if I wanted to be alone, others apparently do, and just once everyone should walk it accompanied by Arthur Lee Jacobson's *Trees of Green Lake*. If what I wanted was conversation ranging from casual to good, Green Lake is ideal, since others leave you alone and the scene provides fodder for the talk. It is a great city street.

18 North End Parks

I n 1945 the north city limits of Seattle were as they had been
since the turn of the century, N.E. 65th, North and N.W. 85th.
Within a decade it was 145th, and areas far north of that
were filled in with houses, schools and playfields, and shopping centers. An entire congressional district had been created.

The growth was monolithic as well as massive, producing
the single-family ranch style or split level house and its "conve-
niences," two to five children, station wagon, "good" schools and
PTA, Little League, strict gender roles. It is a suburban model, and
the North End became Seattle's largest suburb. On the east side
of Lake Washington, bedroom communities have grown up
throughout the postwar era, but eventually the Eastside developed its own exciting economic life, while the North End has
remained what it was—its major business real estate, its major
occupation schoolteaching.

A friend says of her house that it "has a bad case of the 50s."
There is much about the house she loves, and anyone might
treasure its spectacular Puget Sound view. I treasure her phrase,
however. Walking or driving through the North End becomes
monotonous quickly, and even the distinctions it is possible to

make (there are streets with and without curbs and sidewalks, areas where trees were or were not cut down when the houses were built, the commerce of Lake City Way is not that of Northgate Way) do not seem interesting to make, even by those who say the North End is a fine place for kids to grow up in.

Since that is the claim, my chapter title is something of an oxymoron. When you are looking for a "great place for kids," you want playfield, playground equipment, bathing beach. There are almost no parks in the North End.

In Seattle's first boom years, parks were either "breathing places for the Employed" or Olmsted-connected "wilderness" parks. The suburban model needed neither of these. In the second boom years, "old" Seattle made new parks by recycling old used land, but the North End did not want these either.

Along Puget Sound are two parks, both created in the 1920s—one a "breathing place," the other a "wilderness." Both are popular and worth a visit.

GOLDEN GARDENS

Bus: The #17 takes you there, but you'll see that everyone else arrives by car.

This is at the north end of Shilshole Bay, above the state's largest marina. Officially some of the park is on the hillside east of the train tracks, but everyone thinks of Golden Gardens as the beach. If you are planning a trip here, bear in mind two things. First, it permits beach fires and after you get one started you can usually find wood to keep it going, so you can have a picnic here year round when it isn't raining or bitter cold. Weekday lunch can be quiet and leisurely, supper and sundown are terrific. Second, it can be crowded, especially on weekends in warm months, and youths need cars partly to make noise. There is a public fishing dock at the south end, clamming off Meadow Point when tides are low. For dessert, there is the lovely Sunset Hill viewpoint above, on 34th N.W. between N.W. 75th and 77th.

CARKEEK PARK

Bus: The #28 takes you to Third N.W. and N.W. 110th, from where it is a half mile walk downhill to the park entrance.

Carkeek is the last of the old "wilderness" parks, though one look reveals it is not old growth. Morgan Carkeek, an early Seattle contractor (and father of Guendolen Plestcheeff, the grande dame of 814 East Highland Drive on Capitol Hill), originally gave land for a park near Sand Point on Lake Washington. When the U.S. Navy claimed that spot for an air station in the 1920s, Carkeek gave the city money to buy Piper's Canyon, on Puget Sound, halfway between the north city limits and The Highlands.

Carkeek Park has been compromised often since its inception, yet it seems to overcome its troubles. First, it is a ravine, so if it was to have a road at all it would split the forest rather than stay on the boundary, as happens at Lincoln or Schmitz. A road was built. Second, Burlington Northern tracks divide the beach from the rest. Third, the EPA and Metro have a waste plant at the park's edge, and you must get half a mile from it to be out of earshot of droning pumps and truck noises. Finally, the forest is hillside, so the trails are mostly up and down, and the beach has none of the sand of Golden Gardens.

At the park entrance is a trail map, which you need only to get started. Once on a hillside, you are on your own. The mazes of trails can soon make you feel slightly lost and the park seem larger than it is. The forest is distinctly second growth, more alder and maple than fir or cedar, so there is little to engage the tree fancier, but the trails are uncrowded and get really good when you begin to hear bird call rather than sewage pump.

Just northwest of the sewage plant is an archery range, and near the tracks is the city's only airfield for model airplanes.

Once over the footbridge to the beach, something happens. I have stood on the bridge and watched kids, ranging in age from four or five to eleven and twelve, in ones, two, and threes, genuinely interesting themselves—digging for clams, overturning rocks to find crabs, playing in a saltwater pool. Something similar happens at Lincoln and Discovery parks, where the shoreline is like this one. But after seeing what could be the same kids get quickly bored at the locks, the waterfront, and the zoo, this sight is especially exhilarating.

For all but the most intrepid, Puget Sound is too cold to swim in. But Lake Washington is not, and so from June through October, **Matthews Beach,** just off N.E. 93rd (no sign), itself just off Sand Point Way (#41 and 71 buses), is "a great place for kids." Because there is swimming, supervising adults are much in evidence. Matthews is larger than beaches to the south, and usually less crowded, perhaps because of its unspoken rule that no one over twelve swims there.

Northacres Park, between I-5 and North 130th, is little known, because its nice small forest is too close to freeway noise. ***Magnuson Park,*** at Sand Point, is also compromised by noise, this time of its own making, since its most popular feature is a boat launch. Appropriately, then, highly successful rock concerts have been held here.

Finally, a word about the ***Burke-Gilman Trail,*** named for the developers who built the Seattle, Lake Shore and Eastern, on whose railbed the trail lies. It extends from Gas Works Park on the west up past the city limits and eventually connects with the Sammamish Slough trail going down to Redmond. It was hailed as a great triumph when it was created, and a great plus it has proved to be. Except for its western stretch between Gas Works and the University of Washington, it is not much to walk on, since you are mostly looking at blackberries and condos. But it is perfect for bicyclers, who can move through lots of Seattle on its path, and at a pace fast enough that they need not find the topography boring.

19 Here and There

This could have been the longest chapter in the book, since it includes what could not easily be fitted in the first eighteen chapters, and since it almost certainly leaves out lots of excellent places. Some of these are worth going to see, and some are worth seeing only if you are already nearby. The arrangement is from north to south.

NORTH

AURORA AVENUE

Aurora is a *run*—a long, commercial nonneighborhood street. Runs are usually found on the edges of cities, so they are often what visitors first see: motels, gas stations, real estate branches, fast food, signs high in the air.

Aurora is one of the incarnations of U.S. 99 in Seattle. Others are Pacific Highway South (a run that extends most of the way to Tacoma), East Marginal Way South, the Alaskan Way Viaduct, and the Battery Street Tunnel. When Highway 99 emerges from the tunnel it is Aurora, to the north city limits and beyond. Most of what people mean by "Aurora" starts with the great bridge that crosses the western ship canal a few hundred feet up, from north

Queen Anne to upper Fremont. Because this is a favorite bridge for suicides, the guard rails are so dense a motorist can see little driving across it. Everyone who walks the bridge is presumed to want to jump, but don't let that stop you: the views are wonderful. It is positively the last part of Aurora you should walk on.

In the Fremont section the motels barely have a chance to establish themselves when there is a pastoral break. The highway bisects Woodland Park and for a mile you might be on one of Robert Moses's suburban boulevards outside New York, also 1930s inventions. When you pass the lawn bowling green and then Green Lake on your right, the great run begins.

For about thirty blocks what you will be aware of is motels, not one of them part of a chain, each slightly different, all formidably shabby, many being the haunts of prostitutes, pimps, and their customers. Most of that is for nighttime. By day you will note, among the motels, family restaurants like the Twin Teepees and Beth's, places to buy and repair lawn mowers and motorcycles or get a deal on a used appliance as good as any in the city, and a veterinarian people come to from miles away. Furthermore, one can hardly not be impressed with the amazing number of signs, telling you, urging you, sticking their neck or tongue out for you. One does not have to be an expert on runs to see that most have nothing like this.

In the midst of all this, at 100th, in what seems just another small shopping center on your right, you will find Larry's Market. Larry McKinney would like you to think, and with considerable justification, that his is the ultimate in upscale supermarketing and in the most unlikely spot. Larry is accompanied by Oak Tree movie theaters—hardly art houses, but not just another chain either.

Above 100th is another break, this time for the Evergreen-Washelli cemeteries, which stretch out on either side. After that, if you are beady eyed you will see it is not just More of Same. The number of signs diminishes, the motels belong to chains, though hardly Executive Suites, the driving seems less tense until, around 130th, you have arrived at K Mart, the parking lots are huge, and Aurora is just another suburban strip. Car lots are not far away.

The best of Aurora is so bewildering the first time you see it you should turn around and do it again, heading south. I'm not saying there is nothing better, just that, in and around Seattle at least, there is nothing like it.

CHITTENDEN LOCKS

Hiram Chittenden was in charge of the Army Corps of Engineers for the Seattle district when the locks were dug in 1911–17, but the credit should go to city engineer R. H. Thomson, whose name was given only to an ill-conceived and never-built freeway. Thomson secured the Cedar River watershed for Seattle's water, located the major sewage plant at West Point in Magnolia, regraded First, Beacon, and Denny hills and filled in the industrial tideflats, dredged the Duwamish River to make Harbor Island, designed the canal and the locks—and all of these are still in place seventy and eighty years later, and still used.

Thomson conceived the locks as a means of gaining access to Lakes Union and Washington for commercial boats. True, because of the locks Fishermen's Terminal could be created at Interbay, and large vessels come through daily, but most of the locks' customers own and operate pleasure boats, and this has probably been true since World War II.

There are three things to see here: the locks themselves, the fish ladder, and the Carl S. English Jr. Gardens. Probably the best months for all three are between June and September, when the salmon are running and when you can see a full changing of the water in the locks in much less time, because the boat traffic is heaviest then. The gardens are not of the great spring flowering kind; fall is best, summer is fine. But fish are in the ladder every day of the year, you do not have to see a full change of water to see the locks work, and the gardens are always in excellent trim.

You can get an identification map of the garden from the Visitor Center, which you will need because only a few specimens are tagged. There are many relatively rare varieties of common trees, like magnolias and flowering cherries; just near the entrance you will find a canyon live oak, a ring-cupped oak, a tanbark oak, a Holm oak, a California black oak, and others. If you take the main walk west from the Visitor Center, the first path on your right brackets beds 121 and 122, my favorites: a huge crabapple forty feet tall and wide, a number of handsome cypresses and cedar cultivars, a royal paulownia with its handsome purple flowers. Whatever you fancy, a half hour's walk in these relatively small gardens is a feast.

PHINNEY RIDGE

This is not worth a special trip, but if you are at the zoo or in the Phinney Ridge area, North 57th is well worth a look. If you start in the west parking lot of the zoo, North 57th will duck under Phinney Avenue and wind its way down to Ballard, becoming N.W. 56th along the way. Starting at Third N.W., there is a large alignment of six pin oaks, and then, on 56th, the tree of choice is European hornbeam. All this is surprising because the North and N.W. streets in the city are generally not rich in street trees. What you have here is the Olmsted boulevard plan petering out, but doing it splendidly. I don't think anyone knows why it went no further than this.

Above the Wedgwood neighborhood and the Sand Point Country Club, the streets get close to being *echt* North End. On N.E. 88th, heading east from 35th, is a sign for 42nd N.E. just before 88th ends. You start down the hill and you soon are in a different world, forest essentially, houses tucked in here and there. The road becomes N.E. 92nd as it bends right, keeps moving downhill until it stops at 45th N.E.

The contrast with North 57th west of the zoo is instructive. On Phinney Ridge the forest was logged off first time around, as was the case in all pre–World War II Seattle. The oaks and hornbeams came later, though in this case not much later. On N.E. 92nd there had been logging once, but here second growth came in, so it was forest again when Seattle moved toward it after the war. The owner of this land covenanted in her will that those who bought lots must keep the forest; the legal work was done by Slade Gorton, who went on to be state attorney general and U.S. senator. The houses that were built here are good 1950s houses, nothing more. What gives the street its character is the surrounding growth. A lot of the North End could have been built this way, and it is a pity is wasn't.

In 1991–92 one of the original owners managed to break or outlive the terms of the covenant, and had a section of the forest at the bottom of the hill cut down for half a dozen chateaux, identical with dozens that can be found up the hill in Inverness. Not a crime, but someone who soaped all the windows there in a non-Halloween prank might well be unrepentant afterward.

CENTRAL AND SOUTH

A SHORT WALK IN MONTLAKE

Montlake is a solid neighborhood whose house prices are always high because it lies within easy walking distance of the University of Washington. It is decently old, settled, but there's not a great deal of note to see. But try this:

Park (or alight from a #43 bus) near the corner of Montlake Boulevard and East Hamlin. On the southwest corner is the research center of the National Marine Fisheries Service, and your tax dollars there are busily at work telling you to keep out. Between their fence and the ramp leading onto the freeway is a path. Take it down under the freeway, go through a small copse, and out onto the Montlake Playfield, its buildings in the distance. Stick to the east border until you come to paved switchbacks inviting you up the hill to 19th East. Turn right. On any side street here, Calhoun or Louisa, you can see that residential Montlake is mostly a pleasant nondescript jumble. Press on, cross East Lynn and go down into the parking lot of St. Demetrios Church. Up to your left is East Blaine, and something interesting and strange happens here. First, the houses all seem more planned, individually and in groups, than anywhere else in the neighborhood. And grander too, but not a lot. What is the plan, though, or on what is it based? Hard to say for sure, but somehow the word "villa" keeps coming to mind, especially as the English use it to mean something more chic than your basic town house. It's tasteful, but also at least a little meretricious in the curves of the eaves, the fake half-timbering, and so forth. Still, it is well worth a walk up and down. Coming back, you might look in at the community and senior centers on the playfield. And after you get back to where you started, definitely do not miss the small park with views of boats and Portage Bay as East Hamlin turns around past the Fisheries complex and becomes East Shelby.

SOME CENTRAL AREA HOUSES

Parts of the Central Area date back into the last century, but the streets once known as Coon Hollow, known to most of its current residents as The Valley, north of East Union on the Martin Luther King Jr. Way corridor extending to Madison, are mostly from the 1930s and after. Seattle's first black architect, Benjamin McAdoo, did a lot of work in here. Amid several small, unprepossessing houses, 3001 East Denny seems like something dropped down from an earlier time if not another planet. It is only one and a half stories, but is also a full-blown Victorian house, covered front porch swinging around two sides, turrets and party hats on top, and producing fruit trees in front. Look closely and you will notice that the back side was added later, perhaps much later, but without a trace of interference in the original design.

As astonishing a sequence of "ordinary" houses as can be found in Seattle is at 816, 818, 822, 824, and 828 23rd Avenue. They were beloved by Victor Steinbrueck, who drew them in *Seattle Cityscape.* He dated them in the 1890s, without saying how he made his identification. They are identical, small, on small lots, with steep roofs. Not only have they been splendidly kept up on the outside, but there has been some kind of agreement about paint jobs, since it looks as though all were painted by the same painter, who was told to make each look like the others, and also different.

For a medium-sized city, Seattle does pretty well at offering at least urbanized versions of wild things, both flora and fauna. Foxes live on public golf courses, many neighborhoods have their resident raccoons, and eagles nest in some of the larger parks. 2600 East Helen is rarer than these, since it may be the only one

Carpenter Gothic houses on 23rd Avenue

233   HERE AND THERE

of its kind in the city. It is a farm. It had a barn until fairly recently; there remains a small orchard, pumpkins in the parking strip, a splendid scarecrow, a couple of greenhouses, vegetable beds productive almost year round. If the address is unfamiliar, it is on the east slope of Capitol Hill, best arrived at by driving north on the continuation of Martin Luther King Jr. Way, which is 28th East, then turning left up the hill at East Helen.

CHURCHES

There is not one outstanding church in Seattle, and some of the larger ones are both ugly to look at and uncomfortable to be in. The closest one can come to outstanding, I think, are the Ellsworth Storey chapel at Epiphany Episcopal in Madrona (see the first Lake Washington ridge walk), St. Joseph Catholic Church on Capitol Hill at 18th and Aloha, and St. Spiridon Orthodox Cathedral at 1310 Harrison Street, just west of the I-5 freeway.

Honorable mention then must go to three other pairs of churches. First, on First Hill, among the few buildings worth looking at amid the welter of hospitals, are First Baptist, at Seneca and Harvard, a kind of academic Gothic that's good with stairs and entrances, and Trinity Episcopal, 609 Eighth Avenue, a kind of English parish church with handsome stonework. Second, Mediterranean Gothics in surprising places: Mount Baker Park Presbyterian, 3201 Hunter Boulevard South, and Holy Rosary, 4139 42nd S.W., just off the main drag of California Avenue. Two interesting wooden churches are Bright and Morning Star Baptist at 1900 Boren, surrounded by cars bearing people who don't take time to look at this austere Gothic building, and Our Lady of Mount Virgin Church, 1531 Bradner Place South, which houses

Wooden Gothic on Boren and Stewart

the Mount Virgin Refugee Project. The building is made to look forlorn by the immense I-90 scar just to its north.

BEACON HILL VIEWPOINTS

Beacon Hill is a fine, solid middle and working class neighborhood, its population almost neatly split white/black/Asian. But I can find little on it that could be of interest to the visitor, except maybe Cheasty Boulevard, a nice winding street that runs downhill through second growth off from Beacon Avenue at the south end of the Jefferson Park golf course. That, and two viewpoints. The first is unnamed, at the corner of 12th South and South Forest, when 12th is not the arterial. West Seattle, Puget Sound, and downtown are all visible from here but also available in many views. What makes this one distinctive is the industrial area at your feet, stretching five miles south from the Kingdome. Here are Boeing and half a dozen steel companies, the Rainier Brewery, and, above all, the transportational hub of the city—trains, trucks, and boats all coming together. The second viewpoint is José Rizal Park, also on 12th, but when it is the arterial, on the corner of South Judkins, just below the Hospital Pacific Medical Center. This is a small park, and the view is freeway-downtown-Sound, but enough closer to all these than the one to the south to make them seem more powerfully *there*.

GEORGETOWN HOUSE

Except for its being a residential neighborhood in the heart of the industrial tideflats, there is not much for a visitor to see in Georgetown. This makes 6420 Carleton South all the more remarkable. It is a good-sized Victorian, looking as though it at least ought to be a bed and breakfast if not a small hotel. As befits a house that was built in the Mauve Decade, it currently is painted mauve, a color I doubt you could find again within five miles of it.

MUSEUM OF FLIGHT

The Red Barn here, on the west side of Boeing Field (King County Airport) at 9404 East Marginal Way, was not the first Boeing building—that was on the shore of Lake Union—but it is the oldest surviving one. The company was smart to envisage a museum on this site, move the barn here, and engage Ibsen Nelsen to restore it and add a light airy building alongside. Further, though proud of Boeing's contributions to the history of flying in America, the museum has by no means scanted other airplane manufacturers and pioneers.

What the museum offers is, almost certainly, enough material to make this a better facility than it is. As it stands, exhibits are just stuck hither and yon in the two buildings. Perfectly pleasant men in blazers will guide you through this and that, but no sense of history, of people and technology, ever emerges. Likewise, some exhibits and guides act as though they'd love to do something special for the engineer or knowledgeable airplane buff, but as yet that isn't done either. This is a place where somebody needs a vision and a free hand to enact it.

A fee is charged for admission, with museum members admitted free.

KUBOTA GARDENS

The Kubota family were landscape gardeners in Seattle from the 1920s on, and they created a lovely garden, which might be called Japanese/Northwest, near the south city limits, just off Renton Avenue South and 55th Avenue South. The family sold the garden to the city, and it has been operated as a park since 1987.

Downtown, from José Rizal Park, Beacon Hill

Kubota Gardens

The northern half of this twenty-acre park is quite formal, no bonsai but carefully laid out paths and plantings with typically striking Japanese work with large stones. The southern half is relatively undeveloped, but you should not miss the honey and black locusts at the southern border of the garden. Especially because there are no identifying tags, you should see Kubota Gardens on the fourth Saturday or Sunday morning of the month, when a one-hour tour is offered starting at 10 o'clock.

When you're through, go up the hill on Renton Avenue to St. Paul Church and School, 10001 57th South, for a distinctive and little known great view: 270 degrees at least, both mountain ranges, downtown canyonland ten miles away, Beacon Hill prominent on the left, and Seward Park hill rising up right of center as though it were one of the city's great hills. Most of what most people think of as Seattle is out of sight of this view, which makes it nicely corrective.

20 Postscript: Seattle Beer

The terms "microbrewery" and "brewpub" are now as entrenched in the language as "espresso." But when the Redhook Ale Brewery opened in 1982, the terms, and the idea, were almost unknown, not just in Seattle, but throughout the country. Only a few years later a writer for the *Atlantic* dubbed Seattle the beer capital of the country.

Two related things had happened. First came Redhook, then Grant's in Yakima, Hale's in Colville, Pyramid in Kalama, Thomas Kemper in Poulsbo, so that Washington was in truth the beer state of America. At that point the only rival for the serious beers was Anchor Steam in San Francisco. These beers began appearing in taverns, then in bottles in supermarkets, and inevitably some locals collected an array of microbrewery beers and sold no Bud or Miller or other watery lagers. The second event was that the breweries opened their own pubs, served their beers in cask conditioned (unpasteurized) state, and got at least a few other pubs to do the same. So in all these places you can find much better beer than was available anywhere fifteen years ago, and in a few you can get beer as good as you can find in the world.

At present there are five brewpubs open in Seattle: the Trolleyman, 3400 Phinney North in Fremont (the Redhook pub); the Big Time, 4133 University Way N.E. in the University District; Pacific Northwest, 322 Occidental South in Pioneer Square; California & Alaska St. Brewery, 4720 California S.W.; and Maritime Pacific Brewing Company, 1514 N.W. Leary Way.

With such an abundance of good beer in Seattle, it may seem churlish to complain, but the revolution stopped, as it were, one step short of a full turn. Beer to be at its best must be fully fresh, i.e., left to continue fermenting after it has become good enough to drink. Such practice is usually called "cask conditioned" to distinguish it from some process whereby fermentation is arrested, usually by putting a layer of carbon dioxide over the beer. While this has the advantage of keeping the beer drinkable almost indefinitely, it also deadens the taste, a fact which few dispute. To allow the beer to stay "alive," as it were, requires the lines between cask and tap be kept scrupulously clean, and that the beer be drunk quickly. Seattle's major taverns and brewpubs like to give the impression of "caring" by offering a large array of beers, which means that no one beer is going to be drunk quickly, which means in turn a reluctance to serve cask conditioned beer. Some taverns and brewpubs do this, however, usually with just one beer, usually starting a weekend. Since the pleasure of having good beer served in the best possible way is great indeed, it is worth asking after, and most places that serve some cask conditioned beer will be happy to tell you of others that also do.

A fact too little known: one of the founders of Redhook, Gordon Bowker, was also one of the founders of Starbucks Coffee a dozen years earlier.

Suggested Reading

As I note in the introduction, *Seattle Best Places,* by David Brewster and Stephanie Irving (Sasquatch, revised biennially), is a good guide to hotels, restaurants, shops, and all Seattle's major attractions. Sasquatch also published Theresa Morrow's *Seattle Survival Guide,* which contains lots of items of interest, like public toilets downtown, the biggest Seattle/King County corporations, what's at the top of the skyscrapers.

Of the more specialized guides, there is the City of Seattle's *Downtown Seattle Walking Tours* (1985), text by Caroline Tobin, photographs by Mary Randlett; Brandt Morgan's *Enjoying Seattle's Parks* (Seattle: Greenwood), though more than fifteen years old, has most of what you'd like to know about parks; *Art in Seattle's Public Places* (University of Washington Press, 1992), text by James Rupp, photographs by Mary Randlett, is suitably lavish and complete. Of great interest is Arthur Lee Jacobson, *Trees of Seattle* (Sasquatch, 1989), a truly staggering work because Jacobson knows every street in the city, perhaps every tree. He also writes very engagingly. It is not, however, a tree identification book; it's arranged alphabetically by tree, each entry listing where important or only specimens can be found, so if you're standing and looking at a tree displaying brilliant fall yellow and do not know what it is, Jacobson cannot tell you unless you can make some good intelligent guesses or, best of all, make the right guess and your tree is also listed in his book. While I was working on this book, *Trees of Seattle* was my constant companion. Jacobson has also done smaller guides to trees of Wallingford, Green Lake, and the University of Washington.

Of books that focus on architecture, some of the more prominent are Sally B. Woodbridge and Roger Montgomery, *A Guide to Architecture in Washington State* (University of Washington Press, 1980); Victor Steinbrueck's books of sketches and text: *Seattle Cityscape, Seattle Cityscape #2,* and *Market Sketchbook* (all University of Washington Press); two books published by Allied Arts of Seattle: Lawrence Kreisman's *Art Deco Seattle,* and *Impressions of Imagination: Terra-Cotta Seattle,* edited by Lydia Aldredge. For many years now Peter Staten has published very interesting articles in *Seattle Weekly* on Seattle architecture and planning.

Paul Dorpat has published many books, mostly photographs, of "Seattle now and then," most notably three with that very title (Tartu Publications), *294 Glimpses of Historic Seattle* (Paul Dorpat), and *494 More Glimpses of Historic Seattle* (Mother Wit Press).

Index

Streets are indexed when there is significant mention of them in the text. Pages in *italics* refer to photographs.